Contents

Plan of Intro Video

interchange

Jack C. Richards
Deborah B. Gordon

INTRO

video teacher's guide

CAMBRIDGE
UNIVERSITY PRESS

For use with *Interchange Intro* and *New Interchange Intro*

PUBLISHED BY THE PRESS SYNDICATE OF THE UNIVERSITY OF CAMBRIDGE
The Pitt Building, Trumpington Street, Cambridge CB2 1RP, United Kingdom

CAMBRIDGE UNIVERSITY PRESS
The Edinburgh Building, Cambridge CB2 2RU, United Kingdom
40 West 20th Street, New York, NY 10011-4211, USA
10 Stamford Road, Oakleigh, Melbourne 3166, Australia

© Cambridge University Press 1999

Printed in the United States of America
Typeset in Century Schoolbook

ISBN 0 521 55573 6 Intro Video Activity Book
ISBN 0 521 55572 8 Intro Video Teacher's Guide
ISBN 0 521 55574 4 Intro Video VHS NTSC
ISBN 0 521 62965 9 Intro Video VHS SECAM
ISBN 0 521 62964 0 Intro Video VHS PAL

Book design, art direction, and layout services: Adventure House, NYC

Introduction

Interchange is a multi-level course in English as a second or foreign language for young adults and adults. The course covers the four skills of listening, speaking, reading, and writing, as well as improving pronunciation and building vocabulary. Particular emphasis is placed on listening and speaking. The primary goal of the course is to teach communicative competence, that is, the ability to communicate in English according to the situation, purpose, and roles of the participants. The language used in *Interchange* is American English; however, the course reflects the fact that English is the world's major language of international communication and is not limited to any one country, region, or culture. The Intro level is designed for students at the beginner level and for learners needing a thorough presentation of basic functions, grammar, and vocabulary. It prepares students to enter Level One of the course.

THE VIDEO COURSE

Interchange Intro Video is designed to complement the Student's Book or to be used independently as the basis for a short listening and speaking course. It is equally appropriate for use with *Interchange Intro* or *New Interchange Intro*.

As a complement to the Student's Book, the Video provides a variety of entertaining and instructive live-action sequences. Each video sequence provides further practice related to the topics, language, and vocabulary introduced in the corresponding unit of the Student's Book.

As the basis for a short, free-standing course, the Video serves as an exciting vehicle for introducing and practicing useful conversational language used in everyday situations.

The Video Activity Book contains a wealth of activities that reinforce and extend the content of the Video, whether it is used to supplement the Student's Book or as the basis for an independent course. The Video Teacher's Guide provides thorough support for both situations.

COURSE LENGTH

The Video contains a mix of entertaining, dramatized sequences and authentic documentaries for a total of sixteen sequences. These vary slightly in length, but in general, the sequences are approximately three to four minutes each.

The accompanying units in the Video Activity Book are designed for maximum flexibility and provide anywhere from 45 to 90 minutes of classroom activity. Optional activities described in the Video Teacher's Guide may be used to extend the lesson as needed.

MORE ABOUT THE COURSE COMPONENTS

Video

The sixteen video sequences complement Units 1 through 16 of the Intro level Student's Book. There are eight dramatized sequences and eight documentary sequences. Although linked to the topic of the corresponding Student's Book unit, each dramatized sequence presents a new situation and introduces characters who do not appear in the text. Each documentary sequence is based on authentic, but easy-to-follow, unscripted interviews with people in various situations, and serves to illustrate how language is used by real people in real situations. This element of diversity helps keep students' interest high and also allows the Video to be used effectively as a free-standing course. At the same time, the language used in the video sequences reflects the structures and vocabulary of the Student's Book, which is based on an integrated syllabus that links grammar and communicative functions.

Video Activity Book

The Video Activity Book contains sixteen units that correspond to the video sequences, and is designed to facilitate the effective use of the Video in the classroom. Each unit includes previewing, viewing, and postviewing activities that provide learners with step-by-step support and guidance in understanding and working with the events and language of the sequence. Learners expand their cultural awareness, develop skills and strategies for communicating effectively, and use language creatively.

Video Teacher's Guide

The Video Teacher's Guide contains detailed suggestions for how to use the Video and the Video Activity Book in the classroom, and includes an overview of video teaching techniques, unit-by-unit notes, and a range of optional extension activities. The Video Teacher's Guide also includes answers to the activities in the Video Activity Book and photocopiable transcripts of the video sequences.

■ VIDEO IN THE CLASSROOM

The use of video in the classroom can be an exciting and effective way to teach and learn. As a medium, video both motivates and entertains students. The *Interchange* Video is a unique resource that does the following:

- Depicts dynamic, natural contexts for language use.
- Presents authentic language as well as cultural information about speakers of English through engaging story lines.
- Enables learners to use visual information to enhance comprehension.
- Focuses on the important cultural dimension of learning a language by actually showing how speakers of the language live and behave.
- Allows learners to observe the gestures, facial expressions, and other aspects of body language that accompany speech.

■ WHAT EACH UNIT OF THE VIDEO ACTIVITY BOOK CONTAINS

Each unit of the Video Activity Book is divided into four sections: *Preview*, *Watch the Video*, *Follow-up*, and *Language Close-up*. In general, these four sections include, but are not limited to, the following types of activities:

Preview

Vocabulary The vocabulary activities introduce and practice the essential vocabulary of the video sequences through a variety of interesting tasks. They are designed to make the sequences as accessible as possible to beginning students.

What Do You See? The What Do You See? activities allow students to familiarize themselves with the characters and their actions by watching the video sequences without the sound. These schema-building activities help to improve students' comprehension when they watch the sequences with the sound.

Watch the Video

Get the Picture These initial viewing activities help students gain global understanding of the sequences by focusing on gist or important facts. Activity types vary from unit to unit, but typically involve watching for key information needed to complete a chart, answer questions, or put events in order.

Watch for Details In these activities, students focus on more detailed meaning by watching and listening for specific information to complete tasks based on the story line and the characters or the information in the documentaries.

What's Your Opinion? In these activities, students respond to the sequences by giving their own opinions on the characters and their actions.

Follow-up

Role Play, Interview, and Other Expansion Activities This section includes communicative activities based on the sequences in which students extend and personalize what they have learned.

Language Close-up

What Did They Say? These cloze activities focus on the specific language in the sequences by having students watch and listen in order to fill in missing words in conversations.

Grammar and Functional Activities In these activities, which are titled to reflect the structural and functional focus of a particular unit, students practice, in a meaningful way, the grammatical structures and functions presented in the video sequences.

GUIDELINES FOR TEACHING THE *INTERCHANGE* VIDEO

The Course Philosophy

The philosophy underlying *Interchange* is that learning a second or foreign language is more meaningful and effective when the language is used for real communication instead of being studied as an end in itself. The *Interchange* Video and Video Activity Book provide a multi-skills syllabus in which each element in the course is linked.

In the Video Activity Book, for example, the Preview activities build on each other to provide students with relevant background information and key vocabulary that will assist them in better understanding a video sequence. These activities give students the tools for developing essential *top-down processing skills*, the process by which students use background knowledge and relevant information about the situation, context, and topic along with key words and predicting strategies to arrive at comprehension.

The carefully sequenced Watch the Video activities first help students focus on gist and then guide them in identifying important details and language. In addition to assisting students in understanding the sequence, these tasks also prepare them for Follow-up speaking activities, which encourage students to extend and personalize information by voicing their opinions or carrying out communicative tasks.

To conclude students' work with the video sequence, many of the Language Close-up activities focus on developing *bottom-up processing skills*, which require students to derive meaning. The combination of top-down and bottom-up processing skills allows students to understand the general story line of a sequence and the specific language used to tell the story.

Options for the Classroom

The Video Teacher's Guide provides step-by-step instructions for all the activities in the Video Activity Book. Teachers should not think, however, that there is a limited number of ways to present the material. Most activities can be carried out in a number of ways, and teachers are strongly encouraged to experiment, taking into account the proficiency levels and needs of their students as they plan lessons based on the Video.

Although the procedures for many of the Watch the Video activities state that students should keep their books open while viewing, teachers should feel free to have students try some of these types of activities with their books closed. Likewise, a similar suggestion holds true for other activities that the Video Teacher's Guide suggests be done with books closed – students may benefit from trying certain of these activities with their books open.

The richness of video as a learning medium provides teachers with many options for the classroom. Each lesson in the Video Teacher's Guide describes several classroom-tested activities to extend each sequence and documentary. However, teachers should again note that these suggested activities cover only a few of the many possibilities. Teachers are encouraged to use the Video as a springboard for further classroom activities appropriate to their teaching and learning situations.

General Video Techniques to Try

Once teachers feel comfortable with the basic course procedures, they are encouraged to experiment with other effective – and enjoyable – classroom techniques for presenting and working with the Video. Here are several proven techniques.

Fast-Forward Viewing For activities in which students watch the sequence with the sound off, play the entire sequence on fast-forward and have students list all of the things that they can see. For example, for *Unit 4: What are you wearing?*, have students watch the sequence in fast-forward and list all of the clothes they see people wearing.

Information Gap Play approximately the first half of a sequence, and then stop the video. Have students work in pairs or groups to predict what is going to happen next. For example, in *Unit 13: A visit to Mount Rushmore*, stop the video sequence when Susan and Jim come out of the fast-food restaurant. Ask students, "What's going to happen next?" Have students predict the answer, and then play the rest of the sequence so that students can check their predictions.

The procedure for another information-gap activity is as follows: Have half of the students in the class leave the room or turn their backs to the video monitor while the rest of the students view the sequence. Then give the students who have viewed the sequence the task of explaining the basic story line to those who have not seen the sequence. This can be done as a pair, small-group, or class activity.

Act It Out All of the video sequences and documentaries provide an excellent basis for role plays and drama activities. Try this procedure: Select a short scene, and have students watch it several times. Then have pairs or groups act out the scene, staying as close as possible to the actions and expressions of the characters. Have pairs or groups act out their scenes in front of the class.

Slow Viewing Have students watch a sequence or documentary played in slow motion. As they watch, have students call out all of the things they can see people doing or wearing or eating – whatever is appropriate to a particular unit.

What Are They Saying? Have students watch a short segment of a sequence in which two people are talking, but with the sound off. Then have students, working in pairs, use the context to predict what the people might be saying to each other and then share their work with the class.

Freeze-Frame Freeze a frame of a sequence or documentary, and have students call out

information about the scene. For example, have students tell about the objects they can see, about what the people are doing, about the time and place – whatever is appropriate to the scene or their learning situation.

■ HOW TO TEACH A TYPICAL *INTERCHANGE* VIDEO SEQUENCE

The unit-by-unit notes in the Video Teacher's Guide give detailed suggestions for teaching each unit. In addition to these comprehensive notes, here is a set of procedures that can be used to teach any of the units of the *Interchange* Video.

First, introduce the topic of the unit by asking questions and eliciting information from the students related to the theme of the unit. Then explain what the students will study (e.g., mention the main topics, functions, and structures), and set the scene. Give students an indication of what they will see in the video sequence. Next, present the activities and tasks using the following guidelines.

Preview

Vocabulary

- Introduce and model the pronunciation of the words, phrases, or sentences in the activity.
- Direct students' attention to the example, and answer any questions they may have.
- Have students complete the task in pairs or individually.
- Have students compare answers with a partner or around the class.
- Check students' answers.
- Encourage students to supply additional related vocabulary items where possible and appropriate.

What Do You See?/Guess the Facts

- Explain the task, and lead students through the procedure. Model any new language, and answer vocabulary and/or content questions as they arise.
- Play the video sequence with the sound off.
- Have students complete the task individually or in pairs.

- Have students check their predictions and compare answers with a partner or around the class.
- Check students' answers.
- Replay appropriate portions of the video sequence as needed.

Watch the Video

Get the Picture

- Direct students' attention to the task, and read through it with them. Answer vocabulary or procedural questions as they arise.
- Have students work alone to predict answers to questions if they feel they have enough information to do so.
- Remind students that this is a gist activity and that they do not need to try to understand every detail in the sequence. Encourage students to stay focused on the task.
- Play the entire sequence with the sound on. Replay if necessary.
- Have students complete the task individually or in pairs. When appropriate, have them check the predictions they made in What Do You See?/Guess the Facts as well.
- Have students compare answers with a partner or around the class.
- If time permits, have students check their answers while watching the video sequence again.
- Check students' answers.

Watch for Details

- Explain the task. Lead students through the instructions and questions; then draw students' attention to the example.
- Answer any vocabulary and procedural questions that arise.
- Play the entire video sequence with the sound on. Replay as necessary.
- Have students complete the task individually or in pairs.
- Have students compare answers with a partner or around the class.

- If time permits, have students check their answers while watching the sequence again.
- Check students' answers.

Follow-up

Role Play, Interview, and Other Expansion Activities

Note that since each activity in this section gives students the opportunity to extend and personalize what they have learned in the video sequence and the Video Activity Book, encourage students to use new language to talk about themselves and their ideas as they complete the tasks.

- Explain the task. Lead students through the procedure, modeling the sample language and the example. Answer vocabulary and procedural questions as they arise.
- Have students complete the task individually, in pairs, or in small groups as noted in the activity instructions.
- Have students compare answers in pairs or in small groups.
- When appropriate, have selected pairs or groups act out the activity for the class.

Language Close-up

What Did They Say?

- Lead students through the task instructions. Answer procedural questions as necessary.
- Have students read the cloze conversation and predict answers when possible.
- Play the appropriate section of the video sequence, and do a spot-check to gauge overall comprehension. Do not supply answers at this stage.
- Play the appropriate section of the video again. Have students compare answers with a partner or around the class.
- Ask if anyone would like to watch the segment again. Replay as necessary.
- Go over the answers with the class, and discuss any trouble spots.
- If you wish, divide the class in half or in groups, and lead a choral repetition and practice of the cloze conversation.

- When students are comfortable with the dialog, have them practice it in pairs or small groups, depending on the number of characters required.
- Have selected pairs or groups read or act out the dialog for the class.

Grammar and Functional Activities

These activities vary from unit to unit, depending on the particular structural and functional focus of a given unit. In general, though, teachers can follow these procedures.

- Present the grammatical structure, and give example sentences from the video script or from students' experiences.
- Lead students through the task, and answer vocabulary and procedural questions as needed.
- Have students complete the task individually or in pairs.
- Have students compare answers with a partner or around the class.
- Check students' answers.
- Review the grammatical structure as appropriate.
- Teachers using *Interchange Intro* or *New Interchange Intro* should refer students back to the grammar focus in the appropriate Student's Book unit as necessary.

Optional Activities

The detailed notes for each unit give several optional activities that build on the topic, content, and structural focus of that unit. Teachers are encouraged to select from these suggested activities and use them in class as time permits.

The richness of the visual content leaves additional room for teachers to design and use their own extension activities in class when time is not an issue. Teachers are encouraged to do so.

A Final Note

These suggestions do not represent all of the possibilities for presenting and extending the material in the *Interchange* Video or the Video Activity Book. Rather, they represent a sampling of well-tested activities that teachers are encouraged to use, adapt, modify, and extend to suit the particular needs of their students.

1 House party

Topics/functions: Greetings and introductions; introducing yourself, asking for and giving information

Structures: Statements and questions with the verb *be*

Summary

The sequence opens with students reading a notice. The notice is an invitation to the students from their teacher, John Roberts. Dr. Roberts is having a party at his apartment. Next, we see two students, Jennifer and Bob, driving to the party. It is clear that they haven't been to their teacher's apartment before because they aren't sure exactly where it is. They go to the entrance, where they need to buzz their teacher's apartment to get into the building. Unfortunately, Bob doesn't remember Dr. Roberts's apartment number. Since there are no names printed next to the apartment numbers on the intercom, they buzz the apartment they think is correct and go upstairs. The door to Apartment 302 is open and there is a party going on, so Jennifer and Bob go in. It soon becomes clear that this may not be John Roberts's party: He doesn't seem to be there, and Jennifer and Bob can't find anyone they know. When they meet the hosts of the party, Terri and John, they realize they're in the wrong apartment and at the wrong party. Their teacher lives downstairs, in Apartment 203.

Cultural note

The atmosphere in some university classrooms in the United States and Canada can be less formal than in classrooms in some other parts of the world. Some teachers occasionally meet their students socially as a way of getting to know them better or of celebrating the end of the term.

Preview

1 VOCABULARY People

In this activity, students complete sentences identifying people in order to become familiar with vocabulary used in the sequence.

■ Books closed. As a warm-up to the activity, write the words *student* and *teacher* on the board and have students say them aloud. While pointing to yourself, say, "I'm a teacher." Point to individual students, saying, "You're a student."

■ Introduce yourself to the students by saying, "I'm *(your name)*, and I'm a teacher."

■ Tell students to stand up and move around the room, introducing themselves to their classmates.

■ Books open. Explain the task. Then model the vocabulary in the box, and have students repeat as they look at the pictures.

■ *Pair work* Have students work in pairs to complete the task. Then have pairs join together to form small groups and compare their answers. (Note: When students are comparing answers, tell them to read their answers aloud rather than showing one another their books.)

■ Check answers around the class.

Answers
1) husband
2) wife
3) teacher, student

Optional activity

■ *Group work* Books open. Put students into pairs, and then assign each pair a number – 1, 2, or 3. Explain that the number 1 pairs are the people in picture 1 from Exercise 1, the number 2 pairs are the people in picture 2, and the number 3 pairs are the people in picture 3.

(procedure continues on next page)

■ Form groups of six, with a pair from each picture. Tell one student from each pair to introduce him or herself and his or her partner to the other pairs in the group in the way that the introductions are written in the book. Then have the other member of each pair do the same, but this time from the perspective of the other person pictured. Clarify the task and model the introduction for the first picture, like this:

T: Ai, pretend you're Sue. Introduce Mike.
S1: Hi. My name is Sue, and this is my husband, Mike.
T: Good. Now, Carlo, pretend you're Mike. Introduce Sue.
S2: Hi. My name is Mike, and this is my wife, Sue.

■ As students work, circulate to help and to check for accuracy. After about five minutes, bring the class back together; have volunteer pairs perform their introductions for the class. (10 minutes)

Answers
1) Hi. My name is Mike, and this is my wife, Sue.
2) Hi. I'm Rose Smith. This is my husband, Charles.
3) *(Student's name)* is my student. I'm his/her teacher.

---

2 INTRODUCTIONS

In these activities, students choose the correct response to questions and statements from people introducing themselves or looking for someone. They then practice the short conversations using their own names.

A Books open. Have students look at the photo. Ask, "Where are the people?" Ask several students to guess, providing vocabulary as necessary; accept all answers at this point.

■ Explain the activity, and point out the example. Then read through the items, and answer any questions about vocabulary.

■ Have students complete the task individually. Then put students into pairs to compare answers.

■ Check answers around the class by having volunteers read their answers aloud.

Answers
1) Nice to meet you, Jennifer.
2) Nice to meet you, too.
3) No, I'm not. I'm Bob.
4) Hi. My name is Bob . . . Bob Freeman.

B *Pair work* Books open. Explain the task. Model the first conversation with a student, like this:

T: My name is (*your name*).
S: Nice to meet you, (*your name*).

■ Put students into pairs. Tell them to practice the four conversations, taking turns using their own names. Circulate while students are working to assess progress and to give help as needed.

■ Ask for volunteer pairs to stand up and act out one of their dialogs. (Note: If students are not familiar with the "Look Up and Say" technique, introduce it now. It is a helpful method for students to use whenever they practice conversations printed in the text: Students briefly look at a sentence on the page and then look up at their partner and say the sentence by relying on their short-term memory.)

Optional activity

■ *Pair work* Books open. Tell students to work in pairs to make up dialogs with the incorrect responses in part A of Exercise 2. If necessary, model the first one with a volunteer, like this:

T: I'm Deborah.
S: And I'm Jennifer.

■ As students prepare their dialogs, circulate to give help as needed. After a few minutes, ask selected pairs to share their dialogs with the rest of the class. (5 minutes)

Possible answers
1) I'm Deborah.
   And I'm Jennifer.
2) I'm Eduardo.
   And I'm Jennifer.
3) I'm Bob.
   Nice to meet you.
4) Nice to meet you, Bob.
   Nice to meet you, too.

3 WHAT DO YOU SEE?

In this activity, students prepare to watch the sequence by using visual information to get some initial insights into the story.

■ Books open. Have students look at the photo. Point out that the information on the door will be very clear when they watch the video.

■ Ask students to think about who and where the people are by asking, "Who are these people? Are they teachers? Are they students? Where are they?" (They're students, and they're at school.)

■ Tell students to read along silently as you read aloud the instructions and the two items. Then play the opening scene of the video (until the office door scene changes to a road scene) with the sound off; tell students to watch for the answers.

■ Replay the video for students to check their answers. Then put students into pairs to compare answers before you go over them with the class.

Answers
1) a teacher.
2) is not number 302.

 Watch the video

4 GET THE PICTURE

In this activity, students watch and listen to the entire sequence to find out the characters' names. You may want to explain that *get the picture* is an idiom that means "understand the main part or point of something."

■ Books open. Explain the task. Then read the names listed, having students repeat after you with correct pronunciation. Tell students that they need to watch and listen only for people's names. Point out that they will watch again later for other information.

■ Play the entire sequence with the sound on. Have students complete the task while they watch.

■ Give students a minute to check their answers. Then put students into pairs to compare answers before going over them with the class.

Answers
1) b
2) e
3) f
4) a
5) c
6) g
7) d

Optional activity

Books open. Write the following on the board: *wife, husband, student, friend*. Tell students to write the appropriate word – *wife, husband, student,* or *friend* – next to the relevant picture. Put students into pairs to compare answers. (5–10 minutes)

Possible answers
a) student
b) student
c) friend
d) friend
e) friend
f) wife
g) husband

5 WATCH FOR DETAILS

In this activity, students carefully watch and listen to the entire sequence in order to answer more detailed questions about what happens in the story.

■ Books open. Explain the activity, and read through the items. Answer any vocabulary questions as they arise.

■ Books closed. Play the entire sequence with the sound on.

■ Books open. Have students work alone to check (✓) the correct answers.

■ Have students compare answers with a partner. Then go over the answers with the class. (Note: If several students seem unsure about an answer, fast-forward the sequence to the part causing problems. Play the particular scene in question, and then ask students comprehension questions as needed.)

(procedure continues on next page)

■ Ask if anyone needs to watch the sequence again. Replay the video as needed, and then check answers around the class.

Answers
1) 302.
2) are not Terri's friends.
3) Freeman.
4) a friend of Terri's.
5) husband.
6) is not Dr. Roberts.

6 DO YOU REMEMBER?

In this activity, students use information from the video to describe each of the main characters and to identify the relationships among them.

■ Books open. Explain the task. Then read each statement aloud, and have the class repeat for pronunciation practice.

■ Have students work individually to complete the chart by writing the sentences under the correct pictures. Circulate, offering help as needed. If you see errors, point them out and encourage students to try to correct the mistakes themselves.

■ Put students into pairs or small groups to compare answers. Then review the answers with the class by asking selected students to read their sentences.

Answers
1) His name is Bob.
   He's a student.
   He's Jennifer's friend.
2) She's Bob's friend.
   She's a student.
   Her name is Jennifer.
3) She's Naomi's friend.
   She's John's wife.
   Her name is Terri.
4) His apartment is 302.
   He's Terri's husband.
   His name is John.

Optional activity

■ Books open. Tell students that you are going to make statements about some of the people in the sequence. Students should listen and respond with either "Yes," "No," or "I don't know." Illustrate the options, if necessary, by pointing to the picture of Jennifer and saying, "Her first name is Susan. No. Her last name is Brown. I don't know. . . . Her first name is Jennifer. Yes."

■ Use the following statements:

Bob is a teacher. (No.)
His name is Bob Roberts. (No.)
He's a student. (Yes.)

Terri is Bob's wife. (No.)
She's a teacher. (I don't know.)
Her name is Terri Jones. (I don't know.)

John is Naomi's husband. (No.)
He's a teacher. (I don't know.)
He's Terri's husband. (Yes.)

■ Put students into pairs, and tell them to take turns making similar statements to each other about Naomi, Eduardo, and Ken. (10 minutes)

Follow-up

7 NICE TO MEET YOU

In this extension activity, students practice introductions by matching statements and responses, and then putting them in order to make a conversation. Finally, they practice the conversations using their own information.

A Books open. Explain the task. Have three selected students read a sentence from both column A and column B. Then tell students to work individually to draw lines from the sentences in column A to the responses in column B.

■ Put students into pairs to compare answers. Then check answers around the class.

Answers
1) b
2) c
3) a

B *Pair work* Books open. Explain the task: Students put the sentences from part A in order so that they make up a conversation.

■ Have students work individually to complete the task. Circulate, offering help as needed. Then students work in pairs, first to compare answers and then to practice the conversation. Remind students to use the "Look Up and Say" technique. Finally, have students exchange roles and practice the conversation again.

■ Ask volunteer pairs to perform their conversations for the class. See if any pairs can do it without looking at their books.

Answers
A: Hello. I'm Paul Thompson.
B: Hi. My name is Sarah Long.
A: Nice to meet you, Sarah.
B: It's nice to meet you, too.
A: Are you in my English class?
B: Yes, I am.

C *Class activity* Explain the task. Then model it by introducing yourself to the class.

■ Have students stand up to introduce themselves to various classmates. Join in the activity by engaging in conversation with as many students as possible. (Note: It is helpful for students to have a time when they feel they can interact freely without having to worry about being corrected.)

Optional activity

Class activity Students will see how many of their classmates' names they can remember. Books closed. Have students stand up to ask and answer about one another's first names. Tell them to ask, "Are you _____?" and to respond with either "Yes, I am" or "No, I'm not." Tell students to make a tally mark on a slip of paper for each "yes" answer that they get. After five minutes, ask students around the class how many "yes" answers they got. The student with the most "yes" answers is the winner. (10 minutes)

 **Language close-up**

8 *WHAT DID THEY SAY?*

This cloze activity develops bottom-up listening skills by having students complete a part of the conversation in the video.

■ Books open. Tell students to look at the picture. Ask, "Who are these people?" (They're Bob, Jennifer, and Eduardo.)

■ Read the instructions. Have students read through the conversation individually or in pairs, filling in any blanks they can before watching the sequence. (Note: When students are completing a cloze conversation, they shouldn't worry too much about correct spelling. Tell students they can correct their spelling later, but that for the moment they should spell the words they hear in any way they can.)

■ Play this segment of the sequence as many times as necessary while students work alone to fill in the blanks and check their predictions.

■ Have students compare answers with a partner and then watch again to check their answers.

■ Go over the answers as a class, and do choral or individual repetition of the conversation to prepare for group work.

■ Put students into groups of three to read the lines of Eduardo, Jennifer, and Bob. Then have groups practice the conversation.

■ Ask volunteer groups to read or act out the conversation for the rest of the class.

Answers
Eduardo: **Hi**. Come on in. **I'm** Eduardo.
Jennifer: Hi, Edward. Nice to –
Eduardo: **It's** Eduardo. **E-D-U-A-R-D-O**.
Jennifer: Oh, . . . Eduardo. **Sorry**. It's **nice** to meet you. **I'm** Jennifer.
Bob: **And** I'm Bob.
Eduardo: Well, it's nice to **meet** you. Are you, um, Terri's **friends**?
Jennifer: Terri? . . .
Eduardo: Oh, **excuse** me.
Bob: Who's Terri?
Jennifer: I don't know. I think **she's** Dr. Roberts's **wife**.

9 THE VERB BE Asking for and giving information

In the first two activities, students practice the grammatical focus of the sequence by completing short conversations with the correct form of *be;* students then practice the dialogs with a partner. In the third activity, students ask five classmates for their telephone numbers.

A Books open. Tell students to look at the picture while you ask questions about it – for example:

Where are these people? (At school)
How many people are there? (Three)
Are they teachers or students? (Students)
What number classroom is it? (412)

■ Explain the task. Lead students through the incomplete conversations.

■ Have students work individually to fill in the blanks in the conversations. Encourage students to use contractions whenever possible. Then put students into pairs to compare their answers.

■ Check answers around the class, and review the structure as needed.

Answers
1) A: Excuse me, **are** you Sam?
   B: No, I**'m** Lou. Sam **is/'s** over there.
2) A: I**'m** Celia. What**'s** your name?
   B: My name **is/'s** Don.
3) A: **Is** this Mrs. Costa's classroom?
   B: No, her classroom **is/'s** number 421.
4) A: **Is** Mrs. Costa your math teacher?
   B: No, she**'s** my English teacher.
5) A: What**'s** your telephone number?
   B: It**'s** 306-3778.

B *Pair work* Books open. Put students into pairs to practice the conversations in part A using their own information or information that they make up. Remind students to use contractions when appropriate. Circulate to check for accuracy.

C *Group work* Books open. Go over the task. Point out the picture of the address book. Say, "This is an address book." Then ask, "What information is in this address book?" (Names and telephone numbers) Read the model dialog, having students repeat after you with correct pronunciation and intonation.

■ Have everyone stand up and move around the room, asking five classmates for their phone numbers. Tell students to write the names and telephone numbers in their notebooks or address books.

Optional activity

Group work Tell students they are going to create a class directory with everyone's telephone number. Put students into groups of four with one sheet of paper for each group; tell them to take turns asking for one another's names and telephone numbers. The person who is asking the question writes the answer. Then make a class directory by collecting the papers from all the groups, stapling them together, and posting them on the bulletin board. (10 minutes)

2 Lost and found

Topics/functions: Personal items, possessions, and locations; naming objects, asking for and giving location

Structure: Prepositions of place

Summary

The sequence begins with a visual scan of a rather messy bedroom. The camera then moves to a young woman, Sandra, who is sleeping. Sandra's roommate, Anne, knocks on her door to wake her up. Anne tells Sandra that it is 9:00 and that Sandra's flight is in only two hours. Sandra jumps out of bed in a panic when she remembers that she should be getting ready for her trip to Italy. She then enlists Anne's help in finding everything she needs – from her glasses to her passport. Anne calls for a taxi to take Sandra to the airport. When the taxi arrives and Sandra seems to be as ready as she's going to be, Anne hugs her good-bye and wishes her a good trip. The sequence ends with Sandra breathing a sigh of relief that she finally has everything she needs and is truly beginning her trip.

Cultural note

Many young people in the United States and Canada move out of their parents' homes when they go to college or get a full-time job. They often share a house or an apartment with others in similar circumstances.

 **Preview**

1 VOCABULARY   Location words

In these activities, students first choose prepositions that describe the locations of the items pictured; they then ask and answer questions about the items and their locations.

A Books closed. Write the following prepositions on the board: *under, on, in front of, behind, inside, next to,* and *in.* Model their pronunciation, and have students repeat.

▪ Place a book under a table in the room and say to the class while pointing to the book, "Under the table." Then ask, "Where is the book?" and elicit responses from several volunteers. Next, put two pencils on the table and say, "On the table." Again, point to individual students and ask, "Where are the pencils?" Repeat this procedure with the remaining prepositions on the board, using both singular and plural objects.

▪ Books open. Tell students to look at the pictures. Model the name of each item, and have students repeat after you. Then have them read the prepositions underneath each picture. Answer any vocabulary questions that students may have.

▪ Explain the task, and have students complete it individually while you circulate to offer help as needed. Then quickly check answers around the class.

Answers
1) on
2) in front of
3) inside
4) on
5) next to
6) under
7) on
8) behind
9) on

B *Pair work* Books open. Explain the task: Students check their answers to part A by asking about each item in the activity. Model the sample dialogs with two volunteers. (Note: You may want to point out – or remind students – that the words *glasses* and *sunglasses* are always plural.)

▪ Students work in pairs to take turns asking and answering about the locations of the objects. Circulate, helping and checking for accuracy.

▪ Check answers around the class by asking volunteer pairs to give their questions and responses; if you wish, have the volunteers first give their answers orally and then write them on the board for further reinforcement.

(procedure continues on next page)

Answers

1) A: Where is the newspaper?
   B: It's on the desk.
2) A: Where are the shoes?
   B: They're in front of the television.
3) A: Where are the glasses?
   B: They're inside the purse.
4) A: Where is the wallet?
   B: It's on the sofa.
5) A: Where is the passport?
   B: It's next to the makeup bag.
6) A: Where are the tissues?
   B: They're under the dress.
7) A: Where are the sunglasses?
   B: They're on the suitcase.
8) A: Where is the suitcase?
   B: It's behind the taxi.
9) A: Where is the makeup bag?
   B: It's on the television.

Optional activity

Group work Books open or closed. Put students into small groups. Tell them to stand up and walk around the room, asking and answering questions about the locations of different objects in the classroom. Tell students to ask, "What's this/What are these called in English?" about any objects for which the English words are still unfamiliar. Circulate and give help as needed. (10 minutes)

---

2 WHAT DO YOU SEE?

In this activity, students prepare to watch the sequence by using visual information to establish the locations of various objects.

■ Books open. Have students look at the photo. Say, "Sandra is looking for her things. What do you think she's looking for?" Ask several students to guess, providing vocabulary as necessary; accept all answers at this point.

■ Read the instructions. Then model the four statements, and have students repeat. Point out the example, calling attention to the correction. Make sure students understand that not all the sentences need correction. Then tell students to predict whether each statement is true or false.

■ Explain that you will play this part of the video as many times as necessary. Tell students that they should only check (✓) *True* or *False* during the first viewing. Then play the first two minutes of the video with the sound off (until Sandra's glasses are found), and have students watch and check the correct answers.

■ Replay the sequence, telling students to watch the video this time for the exact locations of the objects so that they can correct the false statements. Stop the video to give students time to make their corrections.

■ Put students into pairs to compare answers. Then check answers around the class. (Note: When going over the answers to a video activity, it can be helpful at times to replay the sequence, pausing the video when the answers in question are shown.)

Answers

1) False (The newspapers are on the desk.)
2) False (The tissues are behind the purse.)
3) False (The purse is in front of the newspapers.)
4) True

Optional activity

■ **Pair work** Books open. Put students into pairs. Tell them to try to remember the locations of two other objects shown in the video. Have them write the names of the objects on a slip of paper.

■ Replay the first two minutes of the sequence for students to confirm the locations of the various objects. On their slip of paper, have each pair write two True/False statements about their objects similar to those in Exercise 2. Remind students that they can make the statements either true or false. Circulate to help with vocabulary.

■ Have each pair exchange statements with another pair and write *True* or *False* for each statement, correcting the false ones. Then have pairs return each other's papers to check them. [Note: It can add an element of fun to the activity if pairs grade each other's papers. Tell students to give the other pair a grade of either 0% (= none correct), 50% (= 1 correct), or 100% (= 2 correct), depending on how they did.] (10–15 minutes)

Possible answers

The suitcase is under the table. (False.
   It's on the table.)
The chair is next to the desk. (False.
   It's under the desk.)
The glass is under the plate. (False.
   It's on the plate.)
The radio is on the table. (True)
The makeup bag is behind the tissues. (False.
   It's in front of the tissues.)

 Watch the video

3 GET THE PICTURE

In this activity, students watch and listen to the entire sequence to decide on the correct order in which Sandra looks for her things.

■ Books open. Have students look at the photo. Say, "Her name is Sandra. She's looking for her things." Pretend to be "looking for something" on your desk and in your bag.

■ Explain the task, and read through the list. If necessary, refer students back to the pictures in Exercise 1 to help them remember what these things are.

■ Play the entire sequence with the sound on. Tell students to work alone to number the items in the order in which Sandra looks for them.

■ Have students compare their answers with a partner. Then check answers around the class. Show the sequence again if students seem unsure of their answers.

Answers
4 her passport
1 her glasses
6 her sunglasses
5 her shoes
3 her wallet
2 her dress
7 her suitcase

4 WATCH FOR DETAILS

In this activity, students focus more closely on details in order to answer questions about the story.

■ Books open. Have students look at the photos. Ask volunteers to identify the young women. (Sandra and Anne)

■ Explain the task. Then read through the six items, answering any questions about vocabulary that students may ask.

■ Play the sequence with the sound on. Students complete the task alone and then compare answers with a partner.

■ Ask if anyone needs to watch the sequence again. Replay as needed, and then check answers around the class.

Answers
1) nine o'clock.
2) eleven o'clock.
3) Italy.
4) 807 Key Street.
5) dress is new.
6) isn't in the taxi.

5 WHERE IS IT?

In these activities, students complete sentences about the sequence by using the prepositions that they reviewed earlier.

A Books open. Explain the task, and then read through all the statements with the class. Tell students that you will replay the sequence and that they should complete the sentences while they watch.

■ Replay the video sequence until the key is shown. After students compare answers in pairs, check answers around the class.

Answers
1) on
2) on
3) in front of
4) next to

B Books open. Explain the task, and then have students work individually to complete the sentences. Circulate to give help as needed.

■ After a minute or two, ask students if they would like to watch the sequence again in order to refresh their memories. Replay the sequence as needed.

■ Put students into pairs to compare answers before going over the answers as a class.

(procedure continues on next page)

Answers

1) inside her makeup bag
2) in her suitcase
3) on the television
4) in her purse
5) in front of the sofa
6) on the sofa

Optional activity

■ Books open or closed. Tell students that you are going to make statements about the things they have seen in the sequence. They should listen and respond with either "Yes," "No," or "I don't know." If time permits, ask students to give the correct information for the statements to which they answer "No." (5 minutes)

■ Make these statements and others of your own:

Sandra's dress is new. (Yes.)
Sandra's trip is at night. (No. Her trip is in the morning.)
Anne and Sandra are students. (I don't know.)
Anne and Sandra's phone number is 842-8828. (I don't know.)

Follow-up

6 **TRUE OR FALSE?**

In this extension activity, students work in pairs to practice talking about locations of their own things.

■ Books closed. As a warm-up to the activity, take a book off a student's desk and put it on your desk. Say, "Your book is on my desk. True or false?" The student responds, "True." Then put the book on the floor, and repeat, "Your book is on my desk." If the student doesn't respond with "False," call on a volunteer to answer.

■ *Pair work* Books open. Explain the task, and then read through the model dialogs with the students.

■ Put students into pairs to take turns putting things in different places and guessing where the things are. Circulate to give help as needed.

■ After about five minutes, ask selected pairs to share their best sentences (i.e., their best hiding places) with the rest of the class.

Language close-up

7 **WHAT DID THEY SAY?**

This cloze activity develops bottom-up listening skills by having students focus their attention on specific language used by Anne and Sandra early in the sequence.

■ Books open. Tell students to cover the dialog and to look only at the photo. Ask, "What are they saying?" Accept any ideas at this point.

■ Read the instructions, and point out the example. Have students read through the conversation individually or in pairs, filling in any blanks they can before watching the sequence. (Note: Remind students not to worry about correct spelling at this point. Also tell them that if they don't know an answer, sometimes it helps to read on and then return to a blank to fill it in.)

■ Play this segment of the sequence (with the picture off, if you prefer) as many times as necessary while students work alone to check their predictions and complete the task. Then have students compare answers with a partner.

■ Check answers around the class. Then replay the sequence as students follow along in their books and check their work.

■ Model the conversation or, if you prefer, lead a choral or an individual repetition of it. Then have students practice the conversation in pairs.

■ Ask a few pairs to perform the conversation for the class, encouraging them to use the "Look Up and Say" technique.

Answers
Sandra: Anne!
Anne:　What?
Sandra: **My** glasses. **They're** not here.
Anne:　**Are** they **in** the bathroom?
Sandra: **I** don't know.
Anne:　No, **here** they are, inside **your** makeup bag.
Sandra: Good, **thanks**. Now, where is my **dress**? Anne, where's my **new** dress?
Anne:　**Your** new dress?
Sandra: Yes, yes. My **new** dress!
Anne:　It's in your **suitcase**. Sandra, please hurry! **You're** late!

Optional activity

■ *Pair work* Books open or closed. Have students work in pairs to imagine that they are roommates. Tell them to pretend that one of them is like Sandra and the other is like Anne. Elicit suggestions from the class in order to make a list on the board of some of the items that everyone needs in the morning. For unfamiliar vocabulary in English, students can mime the object; alternatively, let students ask for a translation from their native language by asking, "What's (*name of object*) called in English?"

■ Tell students to use the list to role-play the situation of one roommate looking for his or her things and the other helping to find them. Encourage students to try the role play with their books closed, using the language they learned in the unit. (Note: Explain that when students role-play a situation, they should not write out their lines in advance; instead, they should imagine themselves in the situation and say what a person in that situation might say. The emphasis should be on communication and fluency rather than on accuracy. Therefore, this is not a good time for error correction.)

■ Have selected pairs perform their role plays for the class. (10 minutes)

---

8 *PREPOSITIONS OF PLACE*
Describing location

In these activities, students practice using prepositions of place, the grammatical focus of the sequence, by describing the locations of various objects.

A Books open. Tell students to look at the picture. Then put students into pairs to take turns asking and answering questions about the names of the things they see pictured. Model the warm-up task, like this:

T: (*pointing to the television*) What's this?
S1: It's a television.
T: Good. (*pointing to the shoes*) And what are these?
S2: They're shoes.

■ Tell pairs to continue talking about the picture in this way. Circulate to help with vocabulary.

■ Explain the task. Then lead students through the list of prepositions as well as the incomplete statements.

■ Have students work individually to complete the statements. Then put students into pairs to compare answers.

■ Check answers around the class, and review prepositions as necessary.

Answers
1) is next to the sofa
2) are in the suitcase
3) are behind the chair
4) is in front of the chair
5) is under the television
6) are on the sofa

B Books open. Explain the task, and then have students work individually to write six sentences of their own. Circulate to check students' work and to give help as needed.

■ Ask several students to share a sentence or two with the class.

Optional activity

■ *Group work* Books open. Ask students to call out classroom objects or personal objects that are in view of the whole class. As students name the items, write the words on the board, making sure that everyone understands their meanings.

■ Put students into groups of five or six to play a guessing game. Explain that one student chooses one of the objects listed on the board but doesn't tell anyone what it is. The others try to guess the chosen object by making statements about its location such as, "It's under Junko's chair" or "They're on Juan's desk." The student with the object in mind responds with only "Yes" or "No" and keeps a tally of the number of guesses made. The number of statements made by the time the group guesses correctly is the number of points the student receives. The group is allowed a total of only twenty statements. If the group doesn't guess the answer by the twentieth statement, the student gets 21 points. The winner is the student with the most points after everyone has had a chance to choose an object. (15 minutes)

3 Newcomer High School

Topics/functions: Countries, regions, and languages; asking for and giving information about countries of origin and native languages

Structures: Questions and short answers with *be*

Summary

This sequence takes place in a school in New York called Newcomer High School. The students at Newcomer High School are recent arrivals to the United States from other countries. A reporter, Saida Arrika Ekalona, interviews seven students from all around the world (Armenia, Ghana, Bolivia, Brazil, Poland, China, and Pakistan). Each student tells Saida his or her name, country of origin, and native language. All the interviews end with the students pointing to their home country and city on a world map and then translating "Hello" or "Thank you" into their native language.

Cultural note

The Newcomer Program in the United States is designed to help immigrant and refugee students learn English and adjust to their new home. Newcomer programs have existed in various school districts since the early 1980s.

Preview

1 VOCABULARY Countries and regions

These activities introduce the names of the countries that students will hear in the video.

A Books closed. Write the words *country* and *region* on the board. Ask the class, "What country are we living in?" When students call out the answer, write it on the board under *country*. Then draw a map on the board of the country and the continent or region it is in. Point to the surrounding region or continent, and ask, "Where's our country? What's the name of the region?" When students call out the answer, write it under the word *region* on the board.

■ Books open. Tell students to look at the map. Put students into pairs to show each other where they are from and what countries they have visited.

■ Lead students through the photos, and ask a different volunteer to read each caption.

■ Read the names of the countries and regions in the box, having students repeat after you with correct pronunciation.

■ Explain the activity, and point out that not all of the regions are used in the activity. Have students complete the task individually while you circulate to offer assistance – using the map where appropriate.

■ Put students into pairs to compare answers and to tell each other the names of the countries that they added to the list.

■ Check answers around the class. Then ask selected students to share their additional countries with the class. Ask students to call out a country for each region that wasn't used in the exercise (Central America, North America, and the Caribbean).

Answers
1) c (Note: Many Armenians think of themselves as European, although it could be argued that Armenia is located on the continent of Asia.)
2) e
3) e
4) b
5) a
6) b
7) c

B *Pair work* Books closed. Write the following on the board:

A: Where's (*your country*)?
B: It's in (*your region*).

Have students repeat the question and the answer after you with correct pronunciation and intonation.

■ Books open. Explain the task, and review the example. Then put students into pairs to complete the task. As pairs work, circulate to offer help and to check for accuracy.

■ Ask selected pairs each to share a question-and-answer set with the class.

Answers
1) A: Where's Armenia?
   B: It's in Europe.
2) A: Where's Bolivia?
   B: It's in South America.
3) A: Where's Brazil?
   B: It's in South America.
4) A: Where's China?
   B: It's in Asia.
5) A: Where's Ghana?
   B: It's in Africa.
6) A: Where's Pakistan?
   B: It's in Asia.
7) A: Where's Poland?
   B: It's in Europe.

2 GUESS THE FACTS

In this activity, students are introduced to the native languages of the people in the video.

■ Books closed. Write the word *languages* on the board, and then write *English* underneath it. Ask students to call out names of other languages. Write the words on the board.

■ Books open. Explain the task, and lead students through the list of seven languages in the box.

■ After students work individually to complete the chart, put them into pairs to compare answers. Read the model dialog, having students repeat after you with correct pronunciation and intonation. As students work, circulate and check for accuracy.

■ Review the answers with the class.

Answers
1) Armenian
2) Spanish
3) Portuguese
4) Cantonese
5) Twi
6) Urdu
7) Polish

 Watch the video

3 GET THE PICTURE

In this activity, students watch and listen to the sequence to find out what countries six of the seven students are from.

■ Books open. Have students look at the photos. Explain the task, and read aloud the six students' names. Point out the example, asking, "Where is Sargis from?" Call on a volunteer to respond. Then encourage students to predict the answers to any of the other items.

■ Play the entire sequence with the sound on. Have students watch and check (✓) the correct answers as they view.

(procedure continues on next page)

- Have students compare answers with a partner. Then play the sequence again if necessary.

- Go over the answers with the class by asking selected students to call out the answers. Acknowledge correct answers, and encourage the rest of the class to change theirs as necessary.

Answers
1) Armenia
2) Ghana
3) Bolivia
4) Brazil
5) Poland
6) China

4 WATCH FOR DETAILS

In this activity, students focus more closely on details in each interview by watching and listening for expressions and their meanings in different languages.

- Books open. Explain the task, and lead students through the list of languages and the expressions in the chart. Have students, working individually or in pairs, predict the answers before watching; in some cases, students may actually know some of the languages in the list and therefore will know the meanings of the corresponding expressions.

- Play the entire sequence. Have students complete the chart as they watch. You may want to pause the video after Sargis finishes speaking to make sure that students understand the task. (Note: For multi-task activities such as this one, it can be helpful to pause the video after each item to give students time to do each part; alternatively, you might direct students to listen for only one type of information in each viewing. Stronger students can try to do all the tasks at once.)

- Put students into pairs to compare answers. Then write the following on the board for students to use when talking about their answers:

I think number ___ is _____ . It means

_____ .

- Model the dialog with a volunteer, like this:

T: I think number one is Armenian. It means "Thank you."
S: Yes, I think so, too.
T: I think number two is Urdu. It means "Hello."
S: No, I disagree. Number two is Twi. It means "Thank you."
T: Oh, you're right.

- As students work in pairs to compare answers, circulate to offer help and encouragement. Then go over the answers with the class.

Answers
1) Armenian
   Thank you.
2) Twi
   Thank you.
3) Spanish
   Thank you.
4) Portuguese
   Thank you.
5) Polish
   Thank you.
6) Cantonese
   Hello.
7) Urdu
   Hello.

Optional activities

A Class activity Books closed. Hang a world map (or a country/city map for homogeneous classes) on the board, and ask a volunteer to come up to the front of the class to interview students about where they are from in the same way the interviewer in the video did. Review the interviewer's questions. If necessary, write key questions on the board, such as:

What's your first name?
What's your last name?
Where are you from?
Where is that?
What language do you speak at home?
How do you say "Hello" and "Thank you" in your language?

• After a few students have been interviewed, change the interviewer so that several students have a chance to be the interviewer. If you prefer – or for larger classes – divide the class into groups to do this activity. Classes with students from different countries can use the map in Exercise 1. Classes with students from the same country can use local maps (and omit the questions related to students' native language). (10–15 minutes)

B Books open. Play the entire sequence, and have students watch and listen for the name of the city each person is from. Before playing the sequence, tell students to write the people's names in a vertical column on a sheet of paper. Then tell them to watch and listen carefully so they can write down the city each person is from next to the person's name; also tell them to underline the name of the city if it is the capital of the country. Replay the sequence, pausing when necessary. Then put students into pairs to compare answers before going over the answers with the class. (5 minutes)

Answers
1) Yerevan
2) Cape Coast
3) La Paz
4) Vitória
5) Krakow
6) Guangzhou
7) Karachi

 *Follow-up*

5 *WHERE IS IT?*

In these extension activities, students use the language presented in the unit to talk about the locations of various cities around the world.

A *Pair work* Books open. Explain the task, and read through the names of the countries labeled on the map and the names of the cities in the box.

• Read the names of the cities again, this time having students repeat after you with correct pronunciation. Then read the model dialog.

• Put students into pairs to find on the map the cities of origin of the seven students from Newcomer High School. Circulate to offer help and to check for accuracy.

Answers
Yerevan, Armenia – number 15
Cape Coast, Ghana – number 11
La Paz, Bolivia – number 2
Vitória, Brazil – number 10
Krakow, Poland – number 9
Guangzhou, China – number 3
Karachi, Pakistan – number 1

B *Pair work* Books open. Explain the task, and go over the model dialog. Put students into pairs to complete the activity. Circulate to help and to check for accuracy.

• Have each pair join with another pair to compare answers. Then check answers around the class. If there are some answers that students can't agree on, refer them to the appendix on page 66 of the Video Activity Book.

Answers
Addis Ababa, Ethiopia – number 12
Albuquerque (New Mexico), United States – number 8
Cali, Colombia – number 4
Inchon, Korea – number 14
Monterrey, Mexico – number 7
Sapporo, Japan – number 13
St. Petersburg, Russia – number 6
Winnipeg, Canada – number 5

(procedure continues on next page)

C Group work Books open. Explain the task: Students work in small groups to write the names of five cities on slips of paper. Tell students to put their slips of paper on a desk and mix them up. Then each student picks a city and asks, "Where's . . . ?" Using the model dialog, group members discuss the location until they are in agreement. If groups have trouble determining the location of any of the cities, tell them to consult a world map either during class time or as homework and to report their findings during the next class.

▪ Ask volunteers from each group to tell the class where their most distant city is located.

Language close-up

6 WHAT DID THEY SAY?

This cloze activity has students complete the conversation between the interviewer and the first student.

▪ Books open. Tell the class to look at the photos. Ask, "Who are these people?" (The reporter and a student at Newcomer High School)

▪ Have students, working individually or in pairs, read through the conversation and fill in any blanks they can before watching the sequence.

▪ Play this segment of the sequence through once. Have students work alone to check their predictions and fill in the blanks as they watch.

▪ Have students compare answers with a partner and then watch again to check their answers.

▪ Go over the answers as a class, and replay this section as needed.

▪ Model the conversation and, if you wish, do choral and individual repetition to prepare for pair work. Then have students practice the conversation in pairs, using the "Look Up and Say" technique.

Answers

Saida: Hi. What's your **name**?
Sargis: **My** name is Sargis.
Saida: And what's your **last** name?
Sargis: My **last** name is Sedrakyan.
Saida: **And** so, where **are** you from?
Sargis: I come **from** Armenia.
Saida: Can you show me **where** that is on the **map**?
Sargis: Of course. **This** is Armenia, and this is the capital of Armenia, Yerevan. I **am** from there.
Saida: All right. And so, what **language** do you speak at home?
Sargis: At home, **I** speak Armenian.
Saida: Armenian. OK, so how do **you** say "**Thank** you" in Armenian?
Sargis: *Shnorhagalutiun.*

Optional activity

Pair work Books open or closed. Tell students to change Sargis's part of the conversation to make it true about themselves. Then put students into pairs, and tell them to practice the conversation again; this time, however, they should use their own information. If time allows, have the pairs switch roles and practice the conversation once more. (Note: If you wish, encourage students to work with their books closed if they feel they are familiar enough with the interview to do so.) (10 minutes)

7 *PRESENT TENSE OF* BE
Countries and regions

In these activities, students practice the grammatical focus of this sequence first by completing a conversation with the correct form of *be*, and then by finding out about their classmates' cities or countries of origin.

A Books open. Tell the students to look at the photo. Ask, "Who is this and where is she from?" (Sadia, from Pakistan) Then ask, "Is Sadia from the United States?" Have students call out the answer. (No, she isn't. She's from Pakistan.)

■ Explain the task, and go over the example. Then have students work alone to complete the dialogs with the correct forms of *be* while you circulate to offer help as needed. Encourage students to use contractions whenever possible.

■ Have students compare answers in pairs, and then check answers around the class.

■ In pairs, students practice the conversations. Then have three volunteer pairs each act out one of the conversations for the rest of the class.

Answers
1) A: Where **are** you from, Sadia?
   B: **I'm** from Pakistan.
   A: **Are** you from Karachi?
   B: Yes, I **am**.
2) A: Where**'s** Abraham from?
   B: He**'s** from Ghana.
   A: **Is** he from Accra?
   B: No, he **isn't** from Accra. He**'s** from Cape Coast.
3) A: Where **are** Edna and Maria from?
   B: Edna **is/'s** from Brazil, and Maria **is/'s** from Bolivia.
   A: Oh, so they**'re** both from South America.
   B: Yes, they **are**.

B *Class activity* Books open. Have students look at the picture at the bottom of the page. Ask, "Where are these two people from?" Have students call out the answer. (Korea)

■ Explain the task. Then have students stand up and move around the room, asking and answering questions about where they are from. Encourage students to use the language from the speech bubbles in the picture, substituting their own information.

■ After students sit down again, ask several volunteers to tell the class what they found out about their classmates – for example:
S1: Carlos and Sofia are from Mexico City.
S2: Min Ho is from Korea, and Sachiko is from Japan.

Optional activity

■ *Pair work* Books open. Have pairs choose one of the students from the sequence. Then tell them to write as many sentences as they can about the person they chose.

■ After about five minutes, call on volunteer pairs to read their sentences to the rest of the class. (Note: Accept all answers that students can support with details from the video.) (10 minutes)

Possible answers
His name is Sargis Sedrakyan.
He's from Yerevan, Armenia.
His language is Armenian.

His name is Abraham Kwarteng.
He's from Cape Coast, Ghana.
His language is Twi.

Her name is Maria Loza.
She's from La Paz, Bolivia.
Her language is Spanish.

Her name is Edna da Silva.
She's from Vitória, Brazil.
Her language is Portuguese.

His name is Gregory Iskra.
He's from Krakow, Poland.
His language is Polish.

Her name is Chen Shen Ma.
She's from Guangzhou, China.
Her language is Cantonese.

Her name is Sadia Ashfaq.
She's from Karachi, Pakistan.
Her language is Urdu.

4 What are you wearing?

Topic/functions: Clothing; asking about and describing clothing

Structure: Present continuous with the verb *wear*

Summary

The sequence begins with various shots of people walking outside in a city setting. The camera then focuses on a reporter, Paula Keating, who introduces the sequence and announces that she is going to talk to some people about their clothes. She interviews several passersby, who tell her what they are wearing. The sequence closes with Paula describing her own clothing.

 **Preview**

1 VOCABULARY Clothing

In these activities, students are introduced to vocabulary related to the types of clothing presented in the sequence.

A Books closed. Point to a student wearing a dress and ask, "What's she wearing?" If students are confused by the question, ask, "What's this?" while you point to the dress. When students call out the answer, write *dress* on the board. Then point to your shoes and ask, "What are these?" Write *shoes* on the board. Above these two words, write *Clothing*, and have students repeat after you. Then point to other items of clothing and accessories including watches, handbags, etc., and say the word *clothing* until you are sure students understand that the word *clothing* describes a category.

■ Find out if students know any other clothing words by pointing to various items of clothing and asking, "What's this?" or "What are these?" Write on the board any words that students offer. Provide the vocabulary for any items that students can't name themselves.

■ Books open. Have students look at the picture. Introduce colors by pointing to the blue top and saying, "What color is the top? It's blue." Find out what colors students know by pointing to things in the room that are tan/beige, orange, white, yellow, dark brown, green, black, and pink, and asking, "What color is this?" or "What color are these?"

■ Explain the task, and read through the list of clothing items. Have students repeat each description after you with correct stress and pronunciation. Call attention to the use of *an* before the vowel sound in *orange*. Then model the phrase *an orange sweatshirt*, and have students repeat.

■ Have students work individually to match the items of clothing with their correct descriptions. Circulate to offer help and encouragement.

■ Check answers around the class by calling on volunteers to say an answer and then to write it on the board.

Answers

1) c	11) g
2) f	12) j
3) q	13) n
4) t	14) a
5) i	15) h
6) k	16) e
7) s	17) b
8) r	18) d
9) o	19) l
10) p	20) m

B *Pair work* Books open. Explain the task, and go over the model dialog. Then quickly review the use of "What's this?" to ask about singular items and "What are these?" to ask about plural items. Also point out the language for responses about singular items ("It's a/an . . .") and for responses about plural items ("They're . . .").

■ Have students use a piece of paper or a book to cover the words in part A. Then put students into pairs to practice asking and answering questions about the twenty items of clothing.

■ Call on volunteer pairs to each share a question-and-answer set with the class.

Answers
a) A: What's this?
   B: It's a blue top.
b) A: What's this?
   B: It's a blue miniskirt.
c) A: What's this?
   B: It's a black sports coat.
d) A: What's this?
   B: It's a green turtleneck.
e) A: What's this?
   B: It's a black business suit.
f) A: What's this?
   B: It's a black tie.
g) A: What's this?
   B: It's a dark brown belt.
h) A: What's this?
   B: It's a pink polo shirt.
i) A: What's this?
   B: It's an orange sweatshirt.
j) A: What's this?
   B: It's a brown handbag.
k) A: What are these?
   B: They're orange leggings.
l) A: What's this?
   B: It's a blue vest.
m) A: What's this?
   B: It's a tan pantsuit.
n) A: What are these?
   B: They're green pants.
o) A: What's this?
   B: It's a beige sweater.
p) A: What are these?
   B: They're dark brown boots.
q) A: What are these?
   B: They're black suspenders.

r) A: What are these?
   B: They're white tennis shoes.
s) A: What are these?
   B: They're white socks.
t) A: What's this?
   B: It's a black briefcase with tan handles.

Optional activity

■ *Group work* Books open or closed. Tell students to make a list on a slip of paper of the clothes they are wearing. Tell students to include the color of each article of clothing. Circulate to help with vocabulary and spelling.

■ Put students into groups of six or seven, making an even number of groups for the class. For each group, try to assemble students whose clothes are different from one another's. Collect the slips of paper from each group, keeping them together with their group.

■ Pair up the groups, having them sit in two rows with their backs to each other so that the members of the two groups can't see one another when they are seated. Then tell all the groups to turn around and to take a few minutes to observe the clothes of the group they have been paired with. Then have students sit back down again, making sure they can't see anyone from their paired group.

■ Have one member of each group pick a slip of paper from their paired group's pile of papers – still sitting with their backs to the other group. Tell that group member to read the description on the paper and then to write the number 1 on the paper. He or she then passes the paper to the next group member, who reads it and passes it on until all the group members get a chance to read it. Then tell them to quickly decide who is described on the paper; on a sheet of paper, the first group member writes the number 1 and the name of the person that the group thinks fits that description.

■ Continue in this way until all the descriptions have been numbered, read, and identified. Then bring the class together, and check answers. The group with the most correct answers wins. (15 minutes)

2 WHAT DO YOU SEE?

In this activity, students prepare to watch the sequence by making predictions – based on visual information – about the clothing that various people are wearing in the video.

■ Books closed. Write a list on the board of the clothes you are wearing; also include a few items that you aren't wearing, making at least one of your items of clothing the wrong color. Ask, "What am I wearing? Am I wearing . . . ?" Go through each item listed with the class, having students call out "Yes" or "No." Put a check (✓) next to the correct items.

■ Books open. Explain the task, and lead students through the lists of clothing and accessories. Answer any questions about vocabulary as they arise.

■ Clarify that students are to check (✓) only those answers that are completely correct; also, tell the class that you will play the sequence more than once if necessary. [Note: You may want to tell students that the interviews are rather quick; encourage students to look for and check (✓) as many answers as they can.]

■ Play the entire sequence with the sound off. Have students watch and work alone to choose the correct answers. Replay the video sequence to let students check their own answers, but tell students they will be checking their answers with the sound on in the next activity. (Note: It's best not to go over the answers with the class until you've completed Exercise 3.)

 Watch the video

3 GET THE PICTURE

In this activity, students watch and listen to the sequence to check their answers in the preceding activity.

■ Books open. Explain the task, and make sure students understand that they should look at and correct their own answers to Exercise 2 above.

■ Play the entire sequence with the sound on as students check and correct their answers from Exercise 2 while they watch.

■ Put students into pairs to compare answers. Then replay the sequence, pausing after each interview to give students a better chance to check their answers. (Note: At this point, go over only the answers that are correct.)

Answers
1) a black sports coat
   a black tie
   a black briefcase
2) a sweatshirt
   white tennis shoes
3) a white shirt
   blue jeans
   a brown handbag
4) a red and green tie
   a black belt
5) blue slacks
6) blue jeans
7) a turtleneck
   a vest
8) a yellow blouse

4 WATCH FOR DETAILS

In this activity, students focus more closely on details in the interviews in order to correct mistakes in clothing descriptions from Exercise 2.

■ Books open. Explain the task, and read through the example. Have students work alone to correct any mistakes they recognize before watching the sequence; then have students compare their predictions with a partner.

■ Play the sequence, and have students check the corrections they made earlier and then correct the remaining mistakes. While students work, write the following on the board for them to use when comparing answers:

A: In picture 1, the man isn't wearing a yellow shirt. He's wearing a white shirt.
B: I agree. In picture 2, the woman isn't wearing a blouse. She's wearing a sweater.
A: I disagree. She isn't wearing a sweater. She's wearing a T-shirt.

■ When everyone has completed the first part of the task, go over the model language that you have written on the board. As pairs compare answers, circulate and check for accuracy. Replay the sequence if necessary before going over the answers with the class.

Answers
1) a white shirt
   black suspenders
2) a T-shirt
   orange leggings
   white socks
   a white hat
3) a beige sweater
   (dark) brown boots
   a dark brown belt
4) a white shirt
   green pants
   black shoes
5) a blue top
6) a red T-shirt
7) a miniskirt
8) a tan pantsuit

Optional activity

Pair work Books open. Have students work in pairs to write five statements about the people in Exercise 2: two true and three false. Then tell pairs to exchange statements, and play the sequence again so that students can mark each statement as true or false. To complete the task, have students correct the false statements. (10 minutes)

Possible answers
True statements
The man in number 1 is wearing sunglasses.
The man in number 4 is wearing glasses.
The woman in number 5 is wearing sunglasses.
The woman in number 7 is wearing glasses.

False statements
The woman in number 3 is wearing tennis shoes.
   (Corrected: The woman in number 3 is wearing boots.)
The man in number 4 is wearing boots.
   (Corrected: The man in number 4 is wearing shoes.)
The woman in number 5 is wearing blue jeans.
   (Corrected: The woman in number 5 is wearing blue slacks.)

5 DO YOU REMEMBER?

In this activity, students try to remember specific details about the video sequence.

■ Books open. Explain the task, and lead students through the items; answer any questions about vocabulary as they arise. (Note: If you wish, encourage students to answer before watching the segment if they feel they already have enough information.)

■ Tell students to check (✓) the correct answer for each item as they watch and listen to the video.

■ Replay the introduction to the sequence (until just before the first interview). Then have students compare answers with a partner.

■ Ask if anyone needs to watch the sequence again to finish the task. Replay as needed before going over the answers around the class.

Answers
1) Wednesday.
2) morning.
3) California.

Follow-up

6 WHAT'S YOUR OPINION?

In these extension activities, students say whether or not they like the clothes worn by some of the people in the video.

A Books open. Explain the task. Then students work alone to check (✓) their answers.

B *Pair work* Books open. Explain the task. Then model the sample conversation, having students repeat after you with correct stress and intonation.

■ Call attention to the language box and the thought bubble in the picture. Read through them with the students, answering any questions that arise.

■ Put students into pairs to compare their opinions about the clothing in the photos in part A. Circulate to give help and encouragement.

Optional activity

Class activity Books open. Take a poll (through a show of hands) of students' likes and dislikes, and keep a tally on the board. Ask, "Who likes the black suit? Raise your hand." Continue asking questions like this until you have all your students' opinions of the clothes in Exercise 6. Then have students look at the tally to see if they generally agree with one another or have varied opinions, and to determine which types of clothing are the most popular. (5–10 minutes)

Language close-up

7 WHAT DID THEY SAY?

This cloze activity has students focus on specific language used by Paula Keating and the first two people that she interviews.

■ Books open. Read the instructions, and tell students to look at the photos.

■ Have students, working individually or in pairs, read through the conversations and fill in any blanks they can before watching the sequence. Then have students compare predictions around the class.

■ Play this segment of the sequence through once, and have students work alone to complete the interviews as they listen.

■ Go over the answers with the class, and replay this segment as needed.

■ Model the conversations or, if you wish, lead a choral or an individual repetition of them. Then put the students into groups of three to practice the conversations. Finally, have one or two selected groups act out the conversations in front of the class, using the "Look Up and Say" technique.

Answers

1) Paula: Good morning!
   Man: Good **morning**.
   Paula: Are **you** going to work?
   Man: I **am** going to **work**.
   Paula: And **what** are you **wearing** today?
   Man: Today **I'm** wearing a **black** coat, white **shirt**, black **tie**, and **black** suspenders.
   Paula: What **color** is your briefcase?
   Man: **I'm** carrying a **black** briefcase with tan handles.
2) Paula: **Hi** there!
   Woman: **Hi**.
   Paula: What are you wearing **today**?
   Woman: I'm **wearing** a T-shirt, a sweatshirt, **orange** leggings, white **socks**, and white tennis **shoes**.

Optional activity

Group work Books open or closed. Have groups act out the conversations again, substituting information of their own.

8 *PRESENT CONTINUOUS*
Asking about and describing clothing

In these activities, students practice the grammatical focus of the unit, the present continuous of the verb *wear*.

A Books open. Explain the task, and call attention to the picture. Ask, "What's he wearing?" Have students call out their answers. Incorporate the answers into a full sentence, such as, "He's wearing a yellow sweatshirt, green pants, blue tennis shoes, and a brown hat." Write the sentence on the board.

■ Still referring to the picture and the sentence on the board, point out the present continuous form (*'s wearing*). Underline the verb *be* (*'s*) and the present participle (*wearing*).

■ Have students work alone to complete the conversations with the present continuous of *wear*. Encourage students to use contractions whenever possible. Circulate to offer help and to check for accuracy.

■ Put students into pairs to compare answers and to read the conversations together.

■ Check answers around the class, and review the present continuous as necessary. Then call on five volunteer pairs each to act out one of the conversations for the rest of the class.

Answers
1) A: **Are** you **wearing** slacks today?
   B: No, **I'm wearing** blue jeans.
2) A: What**'s** our teacher **wearing** today?
   B: She**'s wearing** a brown sweater, a blue blouse, and a gray skirt.
3) A: What color shoes **are** you **wearing**?
   B: **I'm wearing** tan shoes today.
4) A: **Are** your classmates **wearing** coats today?
   B: No, they **aren't/'re not wearing** coats, but they**'re wearing** sweaters.
5) A: What colors **are** you **wearing** today?
   B: **I'm wearing** yellow, blue, brown, and green.

B *Pair work* Books open. Explain the task. Have students practice the conversations again, substituting information of their own. Then have several pairs each share a question-and-answer set with the class.

Optional activity

■ *Pair work* Books open or closed. Provide the class with colored markers, pens, or pencils. Tell students to draw someone dressed in colorful clothing. Encourage them not to let anyone see their drawings.

■ Put students into pairs. Tell them to sit facing each other but with a notebook or book in between so they can't see each other's drawings.

■ Tell each student to take out a clean sheet of paper and then to decide which partner will go first. The student who goes first describes his or her drawing, and the partner tries to draw it. When the pair is finished, the "describer" and the "drawer" compare drawings. Have students repeat the process with the other partner's picture. As students work, circulate to encourage the use of accurate language and to help with vocabulary. (10–15 minutes)

5 What are you doing?

Topic/functions: Common activities; telling time, asking about and describing current activities

Structures: Present continuous: statements and questions

Summary

The sequence takes place in the home of Mariko and Vicki, two young women who live together in Los Angeles. They decide to call their friend Paulo to invite him to the party they're having on Saturday. Paulo is visiting his family in Rio de Janeiro, but he will be back in Los Angeles in time for the party. Vicki, who makes the call, doesn't seem to know that there is a time difference between the two cities. When Paulo answers the phone, Vicki immediately realizes that she has woken him up; although it's midnight in Los Angeles, it's 6:00 in the morning in Rio. Paulo tells Vicki he will call her back later. Shortly after saying good-bye to Paulo, Vicki goes to bed; soon afterward, her roommate does the same. When the phone rings a while later, both Vicki and Mariko stumble into the living room to answer it. Vicki finally locates the phone. Paulo is calling her back – at 9:00 A.M. in Rio, 3:00 A.M. in Los Angeles!

 *Preview*

1 VOCABULARY Actions and telling time

In these activities, students are first introduced through pictures to vocabulary that is presented in the sequence; they then practice asking and answering questions about the information given in the pictures.

■ Books closed. As a warm-up to the activity, ask the class, "What am I doing?" Have students call out what you are doing as they watch you pantomime the following actions: reading a book, answering the telephone, sitting down, getting up, and sleeping. Write students' answers on the board, or provide the answers yourself if necessary.

A Books open. Explain the task. Then model the phrases for the students, and have them look at the pictures.

■ Go over the example. Then have students work individually to write each of the actions under the appropriate picture.

■ Put students into pairs to compare answers. Then check answers around the class.

Answers
1) sitting on the sofa
2) sleeping
3) getting up
4) having breakfast
5) calling a friend
6) looking up a phone number
7) reading a book
8) answering the phone

B *Pair work* Explain the task, and make sure that students understand the difference between A.M. and P.M. (A.M. indicates the hours from midnight until just before noon; P.M. indicates the hours from noon until just before midnight.)

■ Read the sample dialog aloud, having students repeat after you with correct stress and intonation. Then put students into pairs to take turns asking and answering questions about the actions and times shown in the pictures. Circulate to help and to check for accuracy. Then ask volunteer pairs to share their questions and answers with the rest of the class.

Answers

1) A: What time is it in Paris?
B: It's 12:00 A.M./It's midnight.
A: What's Nicole doing?
B: She's sitting on the sofa.

2) A: What time is it in Moscow?
B: It's 2:00 A.M.
A: What's Elena doing?
B: She's sleeping.

3) A: What time is it in Bangkok?
B: It's 6:00 A.M.
A: What's Pravit doing?
B: He's getting up.

4) A: What time is it in Hong Kong?
B: It's 7:00 A.M.
A: What's Mei-Lan doing?
B: She's having breakfast.

5) A: What time is it in Seoul?
B: It's 8:00 A.M.
A: What's Ja Yong doing?
B: He's calling a friend.

6) A: What time is it in Los Angeles?
B: It's 3:00 P.M.
A: What's Tammy doing?
B: She's looking up a phone number.

7) A: What time is it in Mexico City?
B: It's 5:00 P.M.
A: What's David doing?
B: He's reading a book.

8) A: What time is it in Rio?
B: It's 9:00 P.M.
A: What's Maria doing?
B: She's answering the phone.

Optional activity

Group work Books closed. On the board, write the names of the people in the pictures in Exercise 1; mix up the order of the names. Put students into groups of three, and tell them to try to remember what each person in the pictures is doing and to make a group list of their answers. For bonus points, tell groups to write the times of the actions that they remember. The group with the most correct answers wins. (5–10 minutes)

2 WHAT DO YOU SEE?

In this activity, students prepare to watch the sequence by using visual information to put events in the correct order.

■ Books open. Explain the task, and put students into pairs to tell each other what they think the person or people are doing in each picture. Circulate to offer help and encouragement.

■ Call attention to the example, and explain that this picture shows the first scene in the video. Also, point out that the sentence underneath the picture is part of the task in the next exercise. Ask students to predict the correct order of the remaining pictures before watching the sequence. (Note: Students should not read the sentences in Exercise 3 at this point.)

■ Play the entire sequence with the sound off. As they watch, have students check and correct their predictions. Then put students into pairs to compare answers. (Note: Do not give away the correct sequence at this point. Tell students that they will have a chance to check their answers in the next activity.)

 Watch the video

3 GET THE PICTURE

In these activities, students watch and listen to the sequence in order to first check (and revise, if necessary) their answers to Exercise 2 and then to match each description to the appropriate picture.

A Books open. Explain the task, and have students look back at their answers to Exercise 2.

■ Play the sequence with the sound on, and have students check and correct their answers while viewing.

■ Have students compare answers with a partner. Then ask if anyone needs to watch the sequence again; replay as necessary.

(procedure continues on next page)

B Books open. Explain the task, and go over the example in Exercise 2. If you wish, have students work in pairs to predict the answers before watching the sequence. Make sure students understand that they are to write complete sentences using the information in the box.

■ Play the sequence, and tell students to write the correct sentence under each photo. Then ask students to compare answers in pairs or small groups.

■ Ask if anyone needs to watch the sequence again, and replay as necessary before going over the answers with the class.

Answers (from left to right)
2 Vicki is looking up a phone number.
4 Paulo is sleeping.
1 Mariko is reading a book.
7 Vicki is answering the phone.
5 Vicki is sleeping.
8 Paulo is having breakfast.
6 Vicki is getting up.
3 Vicki is calling Paulo.

4 WATCH FOR DETAILS

In this activity, students watch and listen for specific information needed to answer questions about the story in the video.

■ Books open. Explain the task, and read the items aloud; go over vocabulary as needed.

■ Books closed. Play the sequence with the sound on. Remind students to watch and listen for information that will help them answer the questions.

■ Books open. Have students, working individually or in pairs, answer the questions. Then put students into pairs to compare answers by taking turns reading the statements with the correct endings.

■ Check answers around the class. If there are errors, replay the sequence so that students can correct their mistakes.

Answers
1) Saturday.   5) 6:00 A.M.
2) Rio de Janeiro.   6) 9:00 A.M.
3) Los Angeles.   7) 3:00 A.M.
4) midnight.

Optional activity

■ *Pair work* Books closed. Have students watch the sequence again and then work with a partner to write three incomplete statements about the sequence.

■ Have pairs exchange statements and then watch the sequence again to complete each statement. (10 minutes)

Possible answers
Mariko is reading . . . (a book).
Vicki is sitting on . . . (a chair).
Paulo is wearing . . . (pajamas).
Vicki is wearing . . . (jeans).
Mariko is sitting on . . . (the sofa).

 *Follow-up*

5 TIME CHECK

In these extension activities, students practice asking and answering questions about time differences between various cities of the world.

A *Pair work* Books open. Explain the task. Lead the students through the list of cities, and ask volunteers to point to each city on the map. Then go over the model dialog. Make sure students understand that they need to work from the time in the previous city.

■ Put students into pairs to take turns asking about the times in the eight cities listed. Tell them to note down the answers. Circulate to check that the students looking at the map understand how to read the time differences. [Note: Each line represents an hour's difference – earlier to the west (left), later to the east (right).]

■ Have each pair join another pair to compare answers. Then check answers around the class.

Answers
1) 3:00 P.M.   5) 12:00 A.M. (midnight)
2) 4:00 P.M.   6) 10:00 A.M.
3) 12:00 P.M. (noon)   7) 10:00 P.M.
4) 5:00 P.M.   8) 10:00 A.M.

B *Group work* Books open. Explain the task. Read the model dialog aloud, having students repeat after you with correct stress and intonation. Then put students into small groups to take turns talking about times in other cities of the world. (Note: You may want to hang a large world map at the front of the classroom and allow students to consult it if they need help coming up with additional cities and their locations.)

Language close-up

6 WHAT DID THEY SAY?

This cloze activity develops bottom-up listening skills by having students complete part of the first phone conversation between Vicki and Paulo.

■ Books open. Tell students to look at the photos and to silently read through the conversation. Have students, working individually or in pairs, fill in any blanks they can before watching the sequence.

■ Play this segment of the sequence as many times as necessary while students work alone to check their predictions and complete the task. Then have students compare answers with a partner.

■ Replay the segment as students follow along in their books and check their work. Then go over the answers with the class.

■ Model the conversation and, if you wish, lead a choral or an individual repetition of it. Then have students practice the conversation in pairs, reminding them to use the "Look Up and Say" technique. Finally, have selected pairs perform the conversation for the class.

Answers

Paulo: Hello?
Vicki: Hello, is Paulo **there**?
Paulo: Vicki?
Vicki: Paulo? Are you **OK**?
Paulo: Yes, yes, I'm **fine**.
Vicki: You're **sleeping**.
Paulo: Oh, **no**. I'm just **getting** up. It's, uh, **six** A.M. here.
Vicki: **Six** A.M.! Paulo, I'm so **sorry**. I –
Paulo: No, no, that's **OK**, Vicki. **How** are you?
Vicki: I'm **fine**. Listen, Paulo, I can call you **later**.
Paulo: No, Vicki. Let me **call** *you*.
Vicki: OK. **Sorry**. Bye, Paulo.
Paulo: OK, bye, Vicki. **Talk** to you later.

Optional activities

A *Pair work* Books open. Have students work in pairs to act out the scene, imitating the actors in the sequence as closely as they can. Encourage students to take turns playing each role. (10 minutes)

B *Pair work* Books open. Have students rewrite the conversation so that Vicki is calling Paulo when it's 6:00 P.M. in Rio. As students work, circulate to offer help and to encourage students to use their imaginations. After about ten minutes, call on several pairs to act out their new conversations for the class. (15 minutes)

7 PRESENT CONTINUOUS
Describing current activities

In these activities, students practice the grammatical focus of the unit – the present continuous – by filling in the correct verb forms in five short conversations and then having similar conversations of their own.

A Books open. Explain the task, and go over the example. Have students work alone to fill in the blanks in the conversations. Circulate to offer help and encouragement.

(procedure continues on next page)

- Put students into pairs to compare answers. Then check answers around the class, and review the present continuous as needed.

- After students practice the conversations in pairs, ask selected pairs to act out one of the dialogs for the rest of the class.

Answers

1) A: What**'s** Paulo **doing**?
   B: He**'s sleeping**. It's only 6:00 A.M.!
2) A: What**'s** Mariko **reading**?
   B: She**'s reading** a really good book.
3) A: What**'s** your family **doing** right now?
   B: My parents **are working**, and my brother and sister **are talking** on the phone.
4) A: What**'s** our teacher **doing**? She**'s writing** something.
   B: Yes, she**'s putting** some new words on the board.
5) A: **Are** you **speaking** Portuguese right now?
   B: No, I**'m speaking** English!

B *Pair work* Books open. Explain the task. Then put students into pairs to take turns asking and answering questions about themselves and their friends and families. Circulate to offer help and to check for accuracy.

Optional activity

- *Group work* Books closed. Ask students to call out as many actions as they can think of while you make a list of verbs on the board (e.g., *sleeping, eating*).

- Put students into small groups. Have students take turns pantomiming an action while the other group members guess what is being acted out by asking, "Are you . . . ?" (10 minutes)

6 Day and night

Topic/function: Daily routines; talking about routines

Structures: Simple present tense: statements and questions

Summary

The sequence opens with a young woman, Andi, standing outside her front door. Andi tells us her name and age and then takes us into her house to introduce her family, show us her room, and tell us about her daily morning routine. The camera then follows Andi around on a typical day while she tells us about her busy life: She's a police officer during the week and a nightclub singer on the weekend.

Cultural note

In the United States and Canada, women have begun to break into some of the professions traditionally held by males such as law enforcement, fire fighting, and construction.

 *Preview*

1 VOCABULARY *Daily routines*

This activity introduces the language for some daily habits and routines, including those presented in the sequence.

■ Books closed. As a warm-up to the activity, write the days of the week on the board. Say, "On the weekend, I have breakfast at 9:00. On weekdays, I have breakfast at 7:00. What days are weekdays?" Tell students to call out the days as you circle them on the board. Then ask, "What are the days of the weekend?" After students answer, "Saturday and Sunday," underline the two words on the board.

■ Books open. Explain the task, and ask students to look at the photo and the six illustrations of Andi. Read aloud the sentences in the box, and have students repeat after you with correct stress and pronunciation.

■ Go over the example. Then have students work alone to write the sentences under the correct pictures.

■ Put students into pairs to compare answers. Then check answers around the class.

Answers
1) Weekdays, I get up at 6:00.
2) I have breakfast with my family.
3) I drive to work.
4) I work outside.
5) I work with people.
6) At 5:00, I go home.

Optional activity

■ **Group work** Books open. Have students use the pictures and sentences to talk about themselves. Tell those who are full-time students to think of their studies as their work.

■ Put students into small groups to tell one another their daily routines, using the six sentences from the exercise as a model. (Note: Remind students to use the "Look Up and Say" technique when telling one another about their routines.)

■ Ask selected students to report to the rest of the class on any particularly interesting or different daily routines that they heard about from their group members. (10–15 minutes)

2 GUESS THE FACTS

In this activity, students prepare to watch the sequence by using pictures to make predictions about Andi's job.

■ Books open. Explain the task. Read aloud the sentence under each illustration, and have students repeat after you. Then tell students to look at each of the pictures and to think about the job as you ask questions such as, "Does she work outside? Does she work with people? Does she drive to work?"

■ Have students work individually to complete the task. Tell them to lightly check (✓) in their books the answer that they think is correct.

■ Have several students share their predictions with the class. Do not give away the answer at this point. Say, "You will find out the answer when you watch the video."

3 WHAT DO YOU SEE?

This activity has students continue preparing to watch the sequence by using visual information in the video to check their prediction in the previous exercise.

■ Books open. Explain the task, and ask students to look back at Exercise 2 on page 22.

■ Play the first minute of the video with the sound off (until after Andi puts on her hat) as students watch and check – and correct as necessary – their predictions in Exercise 2.

Answer
She's a police officer.

Optional activity

Group work   Books open. Tell students that most police officers in the United States and Canada are men. Then say, "Every day, there are more women police officers." Ask, "Do we/you have women police officers in our/your country?" Have students raise their hands if there are women on the police force in their country/ countries. If students seem interested in this issue and you have a homogeneous class, you may wish to lead a brief discussion in the students' native language. (5 minutes)

 Watch the video

4 GET THE PICTURE

In these activities, students watch and listen for the information needed to answer some general questions about the story.

A Books open. Explain the task, and lead students through the sentence. Call attention to the example.

■ Tell students that they need to watch and listen only for Andi's two jobs. Explain that they will watch and listen again later for other information.

■ Play the entire sequence with the sound on. Tell students to complete the task while watching and then to compare answers with a partner. Check answers around the class.

Answers
police officer, singer

B Books open. Explain the activity, and read through the items with the class; answer any questions about vocabulary as they arise. Encourage students to fill in any blanks for which they feel they already have the information.

■ Play the entire sequence with the sound on. Have students check their predictions, writing the name of the correct job in each blank as they watch.

■ Replay the sequence as necessary, and then have students compare answers in pairs. Finally, check answers around the class.

Answers
1) police officer   4) singer
2) singer   5) police officer
3) police officer   6) singer

Optional activity

Pair work Books open or closed. Put students into pairs. Tell each pair to make up and write down two more statements like the ones in part B of Exercise 4. Then have students exchange papers with another pair and fill in the job described in each statement. Finally, have pairs return the papers to the writers, who check the answers. Ask selected pairs to read a few of their job descriptions to the rest of the class. (10 minutes)

Possible answers

She wears a shirt and slacks. (police officer)
She wears a dress. (singer)
She goes to work after breakfast. (police officer)
She goes to work after dinner. (singer)

5 WATCH FOR DETAILS

In this activity, students watch and listen more closely to the sequence in order to answer detailed questions about specific aspects of the story.

■ Books open. Tell students to look at the photos. Ask, "What's happening in each of the pictures?" Use the top picture as an example. Point to it and say, "Andi is talking about her house."

■ Put students into pairs to talk about the other pictures. If necessary, put the following cues on the board for students to use:

Andi's family/breakfast
Andi/lunch
Andi/to work

Tell volunteers to call out their ideas as you point to the pictures. Accept any answers that make sense and are grammatically correct.

■ Explain the task, and lead students through the six items; answer any vocabulary or content questions as they arise. Have students, working individually or in pairs, predict the answers before watching the sequence.

■ Play the entire sequence with the sound on. Have students complete the task as they watch; then tell them to compare answers with a partner.

■ See if anyone needs to watch the sequence again, and replay as necessary. Then check answers around the class.

Answers

1) 23.
2) Susan.
3) She goes to school.
4) At 12:00.
5) She stays home.
6) Friday, Saturday, and Sunday.

Optional activity

■ **Pair work** Books closed. Write the following questions on the board:

1) What time does Andi wake up on weekdays?
2) How long is Andi's lunch?
3) How many hours does Andi work as a police officer every day?
4) Where does Andi sing?
5) What does Andi wear when she sings?

■ Put students into pairs to answer as many questions as they can, and then replay the sequence. Tell students to call out "Stop" when they see or hear the answer to a question. (Note: You may need to model this.) Continue until each of the five questions has been answered. Then have the class call out the answers; alternatively, ask volunteers to give the answers and to write them on the board. (5–10 minutes)

Answers

1) She wakes up at 6:00.
2) Her lunch is one hour.
3) She works as a police officer seven hours every day (eight including lunch): 9:00–5:00.
4) She sings at Ivories.
5) She wears a black dress.

6 WHAT'S YOUR OPINION?

In this extension activity, students give opinions about Andi's two jobs.

■ Books closed. To prepare for the exercise, write these words on the board in a vertical list:

boring
different
difficult
easy
fun
interesting

Then write these phrases in a list next to the adjectives:

2 + 2 = 4
wearing purple tennis shoes
cleaning the house
going to a party
learning a new language
meeting new people

Point to the word *fun*, and ask students to match the adjective to the action that they think it describes. Ask several students for their opinions. Continue with all the adjectives. (Note: You may wish to elicit additional examples for each of the adjectives.)

Possible answers
boring: cleaning the house
different: wearing purple tennis shoes
difficult: learning a new language
easy: 2 + 2 = 4
fun: going to a party
interesting: meeting new people

■ *Pair work* Explain the task. Then write this dialog on the board, and model it to help students compare opinions:

A: In my opinion, Andi's daytime job is fun.
B: I think so, too. OR I don't agree. I think Andi's weekend job is fun.

■ Put students into pairs to compare opinions. As students work, circulate to offer help and to check for accuracy.

 Follow-up

7 A DAY IN THE LIFE

In these guessing-game activities, students use the language presented in the unit and other phrases to describe the daily routines of people with different jobs.

A *Pair work* Books open. Have students look at the photos. Then ask selected students to read the caption under each photo. Help with pronunciation, if necessary.

■ Explain the task, and lead students through the phrases in the box. Model the phrases, calling attention to the ending sounds of the third-person singular present tense verb forms: /s/, /ɪz/, and /z/. Answer any questions about vocabulary or content as they arise. Then model the sample dialog, and have students repeat.

■ Put students into pairs to take turns describing a day in one of the people's lives and guessing the person being described. Circulate to offer help and encouragement.

Possible answers
A musician
He gets up at 1:00 P.M. He starts work at 10:00 P.M. and finishes work at 3:00 A.M.
A teacher
She works inside and outside. She sometimes has lunch with students and writes on the board. She finishes work at 3:00 P.M. She doesn't work on weekends.
A reporter
She gets up at 5:00 A.M. She works for a television station. She works inside and outside.
A waiter
He gets up at 5:00 A.M. He has breakfast at work. He wears a white shirt and black pants at work. He finishes work at 3:00 P.M.

B *Group work* Books open. Put two pairs together to form groups. Have pairs share their descriptions while their partners try to guess who they are describing. If time allows, have volunteers share one or more of their descriptions with the class.

8 *WHAT DID THEY SAY?*

This cloze activity develops bottom-up listening skills by having students complete part of Andi's description of her busy life.

■ Books open. Tell students to look at the photos and to work in pairs to take turns saying what they think Andi is saying in each picture.

■ Have students, working alone or with a partner, read through the monolog and fill in any blanks they can before watching the sequence.

■ Play this segment of the sequence as many times as necessary while students work alone to fill in the blanks and check their predictions.

■ Have students compare answers with a partner and then watch again to check their answers.

■ Check answers around the class, and replay the segment as needed.

■ Model the conversation, and do choral and individual repetition to prepare students to act out the monolog. Then have students work with a partner to take turns acting out the monolog.

Answers

Hi. My name's Andi. I'm **twenty-three**. This is my **house**. I **live** here with my mom and my dad and my **sister**, Susan. Susan is **seventeen**. She's a high school **student**. It's **OK** here, really. This is my room. **Nice**, huh? **Weekdays**, I get up **about** six. Then I have **breakfast** with my **family**. Then I go to **work**. I drive to work. I'm a **police** officer. This is the **police** station. I **start** at nine o'clock. It's a **great** job. I work **outside**. I work with **people**. At **noon**, I usually go to **lunch**. At **one** o'clock, I **work** again. At five, I go **home**.

Optional activity

■ *Pair work* Books open. Put students into pairs to change Andi's monolog into an interview. Tell the pairs to choose one student to be the reporter and the other to be Andi. Have students work together to make the changes as you circulate to offer help and to check for accuracy.

■ Have pairs first practice their new dialogs using the "Look Up and Say" technique. Then have the partners playing Andi's role close their books so that only the interviewers have their books open. Tell the "Andis" to answer the interviewers' questions without the support of the book. Encourage the interviewers to give their partners word clues to help them if they can't remember how to answer a question.

■ If time allows, students could then exchange roles and repeat the process. Have selected pairs perform their role plays for the class. (15–20 minutes)

Possible answers

Interviewer: What's your name?
Andi: My name's Andi.
Interviewer: How old are you?
Andi: I'm 23.
Interviewer: Who do you live with?
Andi: I live with my mom and my dad and my sister, Susan.
Interviewer: How old is your sister?
Andi: She's 17. She's a high school student.
Interviewer: What time do you get up?
Andi: Weekdays, I get up about six. Then I have breakfast with my family. Then I go to work.
Interviewer: How do you go to work?
Andi: I drive.
Interviewer: What do you do?
Andi: I'm a police officer.
Interviewer: What time do you start work?
Andi: I start at nine o'clock.
Interviewer: Do you like your job?
Andi: It's a great job. I work outside. I work with people.
Interviewer: What time do you have lunch?
Andi: I usually go to lunch at noon. At one o'clock, I work again.
Interviewer: What time do you go home?
Andi: I go home at five.

9 SIMPLE PRESENT TENSE
Talking about routines

In these activities, students practice the present tense by filling in the correct verb forms in conversations and then having similar conversations of their own.

A Books open. Have students look at the illustration. Ask questions about it, such as, "What time of day is it? Who's coming out of the house? What does the father have in his hand? Do they live in the city?" Have students call out their answers. Then write the word *suburbs* on the board, and check that students understand its meaning (an area away from the center of a city, but still part of the city).

▪ Explain the task. Then read through the conversations, calling attention to the example and answering any questions about vocabulary or content.

▪ Have students work alone to silently read through the conversations and fill in the correct verb forms.

▪ Put students into pairs to compare answers. Then check answers around the class, and review the present tense as necessary before pairs practice the conversations.

Answers
1) A: **Do** you live in the city?
   B: No, I **don't**. I **live** in the suburbs. My sister **lives** in the city. She **has** a good job there.
2) A: How **do** you go to school?
   B: I **take** the bus because I **don't** have a car.
3) A: What time **do** you go to school?
   B: Well, the bus **comes** at 7:00.
4) A: **Do** you have breakfast every day?
   B: Yes, I **do**. My parents **don't** work, but they **get up** early and **have** breakfast with me. Then my father **drives** me to the bus.
5) A: Where **do** you have dinner?
   B: My friends and I **go** to a restaurant after class, so I **don't** have dinner with my family.

B *Pair work* Books open. Explain the task. Then put students into pairs to take turns asking and answering the questions in part A, using information about themselves or information they make up. Circulate to offer help.

Optional activity

▪ *Class activity* Books closed. Have students call out the names of all the jobs they have talked about in this unit along with any others they might know. Write the words on the board, stopping when you have ten. (Possible jobs: park ranger, firefighter, police officer, singer, musician, teacher, reporter, waiter/waitress, doctor, flight attendant, lawyer, nurse, pilot, salesperson, security guard)

▪ Have students copy the list of jobs onto a sheet of paper. Then explain the task, saying, "Which job do you like the most? Put a 1 next to this job. Then put a number from 2 to 10 next to each job to show your opinion of it." Have students rank the ten jobs.

▪ Put students into groups to compare and explain their rankings. Then find out which is the most popular job by taking a poll (through a show of hands): "Who likes (*name of the job*) the most?" Write the results on the board.

7 Our first house

Topic/function: Rooms and objects in a home; describing a home

Structure: *There is/There are*

Summary

The sequence takes place at the new home of a young couple, Margo and Chuck. Margo and Chuck are washing dishes together in the kitchen when the doorbell rings. The visitors are Margo's parents, who are bringing over some housewarming presents. Margo and Chuck give Margo's parents a tour of their new home, which still has very little furniture. When they get to the dining room, they all sit down at the makeshift table and Margo and Chuck open up their presents – a collection of lovely, if not very practical, things.

Preview

1 VOCABULARY A new house

In these activities, students practice working with vocabulary associated with rooms and objects in a home, including many of the words presented in the sequence.

■ Books closed. Point around the classroom, and ask, "What room is this?" Have students call out the answer, and write it on the board. Then write the word *Furniture* on the board. Ask students to call out the names of the items of furniture that you point to (a chair, a desk, and any other classroom furniture that you think your students might know). Write these words on the board under the word *Furniture*. Tell students, "These are some pieces of classroom furniture. What are some pieces of home furniture?" If possible, elicit names of items of furniture such as *bed, bookcase*, etc. Ask, "What room does a bed go in?" Elicit the word *bedroom*, and write it on the board under the word *Rooms*. Then ask students if they know the names of any other rooms in a house. Add to the board the words that students call out.

A Books open. Explain the task, and tell students to look at the illustration of the house. Read aloud each of the room names in the box, and have students repeat with correct pronunciation.

■ Tell students to work individually to write the numbers of the rooms in the circles. Then put students into pairs to compare answers before checking answers around the class.

Answers

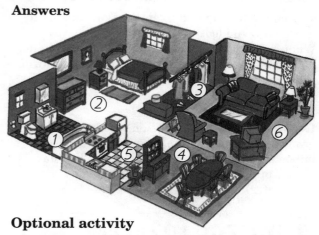

Optional activity

■ ***Pair work*** Books open. Write the following words and phrases on the board:

brush your teeth
sleep
have dinner
put clothes and shoes
wash the dishes
read or watch TV

■ Put students into pairs to match the activities with the appropriate rooms. Check answers around the class. Then, if you wish, ask students if they can think of any other activities for each room. (5 minutes)

Answers
brush your teeth: bathroom
sleep: bedroom
have dinner: dining room
put clothes and shoes: closet
wash the dishes: kitchen
read or watch TV: living room

(procedure continues on next page)

B Books closed. Draw an empty room on the board. Say, "This room needs furniture. What does it need?" Have students call out their ideas.

■ *Pair work* Books open. Explain the task, and present the new vocabulary. Then put students into pairs to number the furniture and appliances according to their importance. As students work, circulate to offer help.

C *Group work* Books open. Explain the task, and read through the model conversation with students. Have students form small groups. Then tell them to compare their answers in part B by having conversations similar to the model.

■ Circulate to help and to encourage students to use their own ideas as well as those in part B. When students seem satisfied, either have them form new groups or have several groups perform their conversations for the class.

Optional activity

Group work As an extension to part C, tell the groups to try to agree on the most and the least important furniture and appliances. Then have each group share their decision with the class. (5 minutes)

2 WHAT DO YOU SEE?

In this activity, students prepare to watch the sequence by using visual information to make predictions about the things that Margo and Chuck have in their home.

■ Books open. Tell the class to look at the photo. Tell them that these people are Margo and Chuck, a young couple who just moved into a new house.

■ Lead students through the list of items. Answer vocabulary questions as needed, referring students back to Exercise 1 on page 26 for any of the words presented there.

■ Play the entire sequence with the sound off. Have students work alone to check (✓) their answers as they watch. Explain that some of the items are homemade but that they should also be checked.

■ Have students compare their predictions in pairs. Then check answers around the class.

Answers
dishes
a television
a bookcase
a bed
a desk
a refrigerator
a stove
a coffee machine
a table
chairs

 Watch the video

3 GET THE PICTURE

In this activity, students watch and listen for the presents that Margo's parents bring.

■ Books open. Explain the task, and lead students through the names of the items pictured.

■ Have students work alone to predict the answers before watching the sequence. Then have students compare predictions with a partner.

■ Play the sequence through with the sound on. Tell students to check and correct their predictions.

■ Have students compare answers with their neighbors. Then ask if anyone needs to watch any part of the sequence again. Play the requested section again before checking answers around the class.

Answers
flowers
a tablecloth
a vase
candles
a picture

Optional activity

■ *Class activity* Books open. Write these questions on the board, and review them with students:

Do Margo and Chuck like their presents?
Do Margo and Chuck really need these things for their home?

■ Have students call out their answers. If possible, have students give reasons for their answers. (5 minutes)

4 WATCH FOR DETAILS

In this activity, students watch and listen more closely to the sequence in order to identify the words that Margo's parents use to describe the new house.

■ Books closed. Ask students, "Do you like Margo and Chuck's house?" Have students call out their answers. Then put the following adjectives on the board:

big
small
nice
different
interesting
great

Ask selected students to choose from the words on the board or to use their own ideas to describe the house.

■ Books open. Explain the task, and read through the six items. Answer any questions about vocabulary.

■ Have students predict as many answers as they can and then compare predictions with other students.

■ Play the sequence with the sound on. Have students correct their predictions, checking (✓) the correct word in each item as they watch.

■ Replay the sequence as necessary, and then have students compare answers in pairs. Check answers around the class.

Answers

1) lovely.
2) nice.
3) comfortable.
4) sunny.
5) big.
6) nice.

Optional activity

■ Books open or closed. Tell students to write down the names of the rooms in Margo and Chuck's house. (Note: If necessary, refer students back to Exercise 1A for help.)

■ Have students work alone to recall the order in which Margo and Chuck show the rooms to their visitors. Tell them to number the rooms chronologically from 1 to 6.

■ Have students compare answers with a partner. Then play the entire sequence so that students can check and correct their answers individually. Finally, check answers around the class. (10 minutes)

Answers

1	living room	4	bathroom
2	bedroom	5	kitchen
3	closet	6	dining room

5 WHAT'S YOUR OPINION?

In this activity, students decide which household items Margo and Chuck still need.

■ Books open. Explain the task, making sure students understand that they should answer according to their own opinions; point out that there are no "right" or "wrong" answers.

■ Have students work alone to check (✓) the things that they think Margo and Chuck really need. Encourage students to focus on things that are important for day-to-day living.

■ Model the partial dialog. Then put students into pairs to compare answers, using the dialog as a model. Tell students to take turns giving their opinions about what Margo and Chuck still need, and encourage them to give reasons for their opinions when possible.

■ Have selected pairs share their ideas with the class.

6 ROLE PLAY

The first activity has students think up and write four questions to ask Margo and Chuck about their house. In the second activity, students are encouraged to be creative as they recall details from the sequence.

A Books open. Explain the task, and lead students through the examples.

■ Have students work alone to write their own questions to ask Margo and Chuck. Move around the room, and provide help with vocabulary and structure as needed. Then ask a few volunteers to share some questions with the class. Accept any questions that are logical and grammatically correct.

Possible answers
3) Do you have a dining room?
4) Is there a sofa in your living room?
5) Do you have a big kitchen?
6) How many bathrooms do you have?

B Group work Explain the task. Then have a volunteer read the statement in the speech bubble above the photos of Chuck and Margo.

■ Lead students through the model conversation, giving them a chance to practice the questions and responses chorally and individually.

■ Put students into groups of four. Tell each group to choose two students to play the roles of Margo and Chuck. Tell the other two students to take turns asking "Margo" and "Chuck" their questions. Then have students exchange roles and repeat the process.

■ Have several groups each share a question-and-answer set with the class.

Optional activity

■ *Pair work* Books open or closed. Tell students to think about the house or apartment of their dreams.

■ Put students into pairs to take turns asking their questions from part A and answering with information about their dream homes. Finally, have several volunteer pairs perform their interviews for the class. (10–15 minutes)

7 WHAT DID THEY SAY?

This cloze activity develops bottom-up listening skills by having students complete the first part of the conversation among Margo, Chuck, and Margo's parents.

■ Books open. Tell students to look at the photos. Ask, "Does Margo know her parents are coming for a visit?" (No, she doesn't.) Then ask, "How do we know?" (Margo's greeting to her parents is "Mom! Dad! What a surprise!")

■ Have students, working individually or in pairs, fill in any blanks they can before watching.

■ Play this segment of the sequence as many times as necessary while students work alone to fill in the blanks and check their predictions.

■ Have students compare answers with a partner and then watch again to check their answers.

■ Model the conversation, and do choral and/or individual repetition to prepare for group work. Then have students practice the conversation in groups of four.

Answers
Margo: I'll get it.
Chuck: **Good.**
Margo: Mom! Dad! What a **surprise!**
Mother: Hi, honey. **How** are you? **How's** Chuck? **These** are for you.
Margo: Thank you. They're beautiful! And we're **fine.** Please **come** in.
Father: We were out in the **car** –
Mother: And we thought, "Let's go **visit** Margo and Chuck and **see** their new **house.**"
Father: And your **house** is . . . well, lovely.
Chuck: Mom! Dad! **Hi.** How are you?
Mother: Hi, Chuck. **Fine,** thanks.
Father: Hi, Chuck. Congratulations on the **new** house. It's **perfect.**
Chuck: **Thanks.**
Margo: Well, let me show you around.

Optional activity

Group work Books open. Have groups act out the conversation, using as many of the characters' gestures, movements, and facial expressions as possible. (10 minutes)

8 THERE IS/THERE ARE
Describing a home

In these extension activities, students work with statements using *there is/there are* – the grammatical focus of the sequence.

A Books closed. Ask students, "How many rooms are there in Margo and Chuck's house?" After students call out their ideas, write on the board:

There are five rooms in Margo and Chuck's house.

Then ask, "How many bathrooms are there?" Wait for several students to answer. Then write on the board:

There's one bathroom in Margo and Chuck's house.

■ Underline *there are* and *there's*. Ask, "Is there a sofa in Margo and Chuck's house? Are there curtains?" Again, write the full-sentence answers on the board:

No, there isn't. There's no sofa. OR There isn't a sofa.
No, there aren't. There are no curtains. OR There aren't any curtains.

■ Explain the task, and lead students through the sentences. Answer any vocabulary and/or comprehension questions. [Note: Point out that the word *but* signals a contrast, and that *any* in a statement is preceded by a negative form (*there isn't/aren't any*). Also explain that if the first part of a "but" sentence is affirmative, the second part will be negative.]

■ Have students fill in the blanks with the correct forms of *there is/there are*. Circulate to offer help as needed.

■ Put students into pairs to compare answers. Then check answers around the class, and review as necessary.

Answers
1) **There are** eight rooms in our house, and **there's** a garage, too.
2) **There are** some trees in the yard, but **there aren't** any flowers.
3) **There are** some armchairs in the living room, and **there's** a large table in the dining room.
4) **There aren't** any pictures in the dining room, but **there are** some in the living room.
5) **There are** a stove and a refrigerator in the kitchen, but **there's** no microwave oven.
6) **There are** three bedrooms in the house, and **there's** one bathroom.

B Books open. Explain the task. Have students work alone to rewrite the sentences, substituting information about their own homes. Circulate to offer help and to check for accuracy.

■ Put students into pairs to compare answers. Check answers around the class, accepting all answers that make sense and are grammatically correct.

Optional activity

■ *Group work* Books closed. Have students work in small groups to write sentences about the classroom, using *there's*, *there are*, and *there aren't*. Tell the groups that they have five minutes to write down their sentences. (Note: Either have groups appoint a secretary to write down their sentences or tell each group member to write down the sentences as they are suggested.)

■ When time is up, find out which group(s) came up with the most sentences. Groups take turns reading their sentences aloud for the rest of the class. (10 minutes)

While the city sleeps

Topic/function: Jobs; talking about work and school

Structure: Simple present tense: summary

Summary

The sequence opens with a reporter introducing the topic of working at night. The reporter proceeds to interview six people with very different types of occupations – from a doctor to a janitor. Each person tells the reporter about his or her job: what it entails, starting and finishing times, and whether or not he or she likes working at night.

Cultural note

One of the people interviewed is a young man who is a university student. It is quite common for university students in the United States and Canada to have jobs to help pay for their tuition and living expenses. Students usually either work part time and study full time, or vice versa.

Preview

1 VOCABULARY Jobs

In these activities, students are introduced to vocabulary related to occupations presented in the sequence.

■ Books closed. As a warm-up to the activity, ask the class, "What's my job?" Have students call out the answer: "You're a teacher." Write *teacher* on the board under the heading *Jobs*. Then ask students to call out the words for other jobs that they might know; write these on the board as well.

A Books open. Explain the task. Then model the vocabulary in the box, and have students repeat after you.

■ Have students work individually to complete the task. Then have them compare answers in pairs before checking answers around the class.

Answers

1) police officer
2) baker
3) doctor
4) editor
5) janitor
6) security guard
7) nurse

B *Pair work* Books open. Explain the activity, and lead students through the sentences in the box. Then model the sample conversation.

■ Put students into pairs to take turns choosing and describing a job and guessing what it is. As pairs work, walk around the room to offer help and to check for accuracy. Pay close attention to students' stress and intonation.

Possible answers

A: I wear a uniform.
B: Are you a police officer?
A: Yes, I am./No, I'm a security guard.

A: I work in an office. I sit all day.
B: Are you an editor?
A: Yes, I am.

A: I work in an office. I stand all night.
B: Are you a janitor?
A: Yes, I am.

A: I work in a hospital.
B: Are you a nurse?
A: Yes, I am./No, I'm a doctor.

A: I work in a restaurant.
B: Are you a baker?
A: Yes, I am.

2 WHAT DO YOU SEE?

In this activity, students prepare to watch the sequence by using visual information to determine the job of each person interviewed.

■ Books open. Explain the task. Tell students to look closely at the six photos and to try to guess what each person does.

■ Have students report their predictions to the class. Accept all answers at this point.

■ Play the entire sequence without sound as students watch and check their predictions. (Note: You may wish to point out that there are no concrete visual clues as to the occupation of the last man interviewed. Encourage students to take a guess based on the man's clothes.)

■ Tell students that they will find out if their predictions are correct in the next activity.

Optional activity

■ *Group work* Books open. Tell students, "Look again at the pictures in Exercise 2. Who looks happy with his or her job?"

■ Put students into small groups to talk about the question and to make a list of the people who seem happy with their jobs. Tell students to check their list later when they watch the video again with the sound on.

 Watch the video

3 GET THE PICTURE

In the first activity, students watch and listen to the sequence in order to check the predictions they made in the preceding exercise. In the second activity, they watch and listen for starting and finishing times of each person's job.

A Books open. Explain the task, and make sure students understand that they should look at their answers to Exercise 2 in order to check their predictions as they watch the sequence.

■ Play the entire sequence with the sound on as students complete the task. Then have selected students provide the answers, and replay the sequence as necessary.

Answers

1) doctor
2) security guard
3) editor
4) police officer
5) baker
6) janitor/student

B Books closed. To prepare students for the activity, write these phrases on the board:

in the morning
in the afternoon
at night

Ask the class, "When do these people work?" Hold up your book, and point to the photos in Exercise 2; have students call out their answer for each person pictured. (They all work at night.)

■ Books open. Explain the task, and lead students through the chart.

■ Play the entire sequence with the sound on. Tell students to watch and listen for the times each person starts and finishes work. As students watch, they should work alone to complete the chart. Then have them compare answers in pairs or small groups.

■ Ask if anyone needs to watch the sequence again, and replay it if necessary before going over the answers with the class.

Answers

Miguel: 6:00 P.M., 8:00 A.M.
Joe: 3:00 P.M., 11:00 P.M.
Hylaria: 4:00 P.M., 1:30 A.M.
Scott: 3:00 P.M., 11:00 P.M.
Eric: midnight, 7:00 A.M.
Steve: 10:00 P.M., 6:00 A.M.

Optional activity

■ Books open. Ask the class, "Who works the most hours, and who works the fewest?" (Note: Clarify *the most* and *the fewest* as necessary.) Have students work individually to calculate the answer. Call on selected students around the class to answer. (Miguel works the most, and Eric works the fewest.)

■ Lead a class discussion on the number of hours that most doctors, security guards, editors, police officers, bakers, and janitors work in students' country/countries.

4 WATCH FOR DETAILS

In this activity, students focus more closely on details in the documentary by watching and listening for information about the people's jobs.

- Books open. Explain the task, and read through the items with the class.

- Play the video sequence, and have students check (✓) the correct answers as they watch.

- Replay the sequence if needed, and then have students compare their answers with a partner. Check answers around the class.

Answers
1) likes
2) tiring
3) talks
4) newspaper
5) newspaper
6) doesn't like
7) safe
8) works
9) stands
10) chocolate
11) in an office
12) student

Optional activity

- *Pair work* Books open. Put students into pairs to talk about any other details that they can remember about the people in the video. Tell them to write three incomplete statements like the ones in Exercise 4 based on the details that they remember.

- Have pairs exchange statements with another pair to complete one another's statements. Then tell students to return the papers to the writers of the statements. The writers check the papers. Find out how many pairs were able to complete all three statements correctly. (10–15 minutes)

Possible answers
The hospital is always . . . (busy).
The reporter talks to Joe at . . . (midnight).
Hylaria's last name is . . . (Perez).
Scott's job is sometimes . . . (dangerous).
Eric makes . . . (donuts).
Steve cleans . . . (offices).

Follow-up

5 ROLE PLAY

In this extension activity, students build on what they have learned about the occupations in the documentary by taking turns playing the roles of the reporter and the people talking about their jobs.

- *Pair work* Books open. Explain the task, and lead students through the descriptive adjectives in the box. Then model the sample conversation, having students repeat after you with correct pronunciation and intonation. Discuss any vocabulary and/or content questions.

- Put students into pairs to role-play interviews between the reporter and each of the people in the sequence. As pairs work, circulate to offer help as needed and to check for accuracy. Encourage students to give their real opinions of the jobs from the sequence.

- Have selected pairs perform their role plays in front of the class.

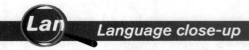
Language close-up

6 WHAT DID THEY SAY?

This cloze activity develops bottom-up listening skills by having students complete the first interview – between the reporter and Dr. Miguel West.

- Books open. Tell students to look at the photos and to silently read through the conversation. Have students, working alone or with a partner, fill in any blanks they can before watching the sequence.

- Play this segment of the sequence as many times as necessary while students work alone to check their predictions and fill in the remaining blanks. Then have students compare answers with a partner.

■ Go over the answers with the class. Then replay the segment as students follow along in their books and check their work.

■ Model the interview and, if you wish, lead a choral or an individual repetition of it. Then have students practice the conversation in pairs, reminding them to use the "Look Up and Say" technique. Finally, have selected pairs perform the interview for the class.

Answers

Reporter: Excuse me. Can I **ask** you a few **questions**?

Doctor: Yes.

Reporter: Are you a **nurse** or a **doctor**?

Doctor: I'm a **doctor**. My **name** is Dr. Miguel West.

Reporter: Dr. West, **when** do you **start** work?

Doctor: I **start** work at 6:00 P.M. in the **evening**, and we work through till 8:00 A.M. in the **morning**.

Reporter: Do you **like** working at **night**?

Doctor: I **like** it, but it can **be** tiring sometimes.

Reporter: Is it busy at **night**?

Doctor: It's pretty busy.

Reporter: **What** do you do, exactly?

Doctor: I'm the **doctor** in the emergency department.

Optional activity

■ *Pair work* Books open. Put students into pairs, and tell them to choose one of the other people from the video (Joe, Hylaria, Scott, Eric, or Steve). Tell them to rewrite the interview to fit the other person. Circulate to offer help and to encourage students to be creative.

■ Have pairs practice their new interviews. Then ask selected pairs to perform for the rest of the class. (10–15 minutes)

7 SIMPLE PRESENT TENSE
Talking about work and school

In these activities, students practice the grammatical focus of the unit – the simple present tense, both statements and questions – first by filling in the correct verb forms in two conversations and then by asking and answering questions about themselves.

A Books open. Call attention to the picture, and ask, "Where are these people?" (At school) "Why is this student sleeping?" Have students call out their ideas. (Maybe he works at night, so he's tired.)

■ Explain the task, and go over the examples. Have students work alone to fill in the blanks in the conversations. Circulate to offer help and to check for accuracy.

■ Put students into pairs to compare answers. Then check answers around the class, and review the simple present tense as needed.

■ After students practice the conversations in pairs, ask selected pairs to act them out for the rest of the class.

Answers

1) A: **Does** Steve **work** at night?
   B: Yes, he **does**. He **goes** to school and **does** his homework during the day.
   A: When **does** he **sleep**?
   B: That's a good question!
2) A: Where **do** Joe and Hylaria **work**?
   B: They **work** at a newspaper.
   A: What **do** they **do**, exactly?
   B: Joe **watches** people at the door, and Hylaria **writes** on a computer.

B *Pair work* Books open. Explain the task, and lead students through the questions. Answer any vocabulary and/or content questions.

■ Put students into pairs, and tell them to take turns asking and answering the questions. Circulate to offer help and to check for accuracy. (Note: If time allows, ask volunteers to share any interesting or unusual information that they learned about their partner.)

(see next page for an optional activity)

Optional activity

■ *Group work* Books open or closed. Write the following headings on the board:

Wear a uniform
Work inside
Work outside
Work with people
Work with a computer
Stand at work
Sit at work

■ Put students into small groups, and tell them to choose a group secretary. Explain the task: Students think up as many jobs as they can for each category listed on the board. Explain that jobs can be listed in more than one category. Each group secretary writes down his or her group's ideas. Set a time limit of ten minutes.

■ When time is up, bring the class back together and find out which group had the most jobs in each category. (15–20 minutes)

Possible answers
Wear a uniform: police officer, firefighter, security guard, flight attendant, waiter/waitress
Work inside: waiter/waitress, editor, secretary, receptionist, lawyer, doctor, nurse, musician, chef
Work outside: police officer, firefighter, security guard, park ranger
Work with people: police officer, receptionist, doctor, nurse, lawyer, salesperson, cashier, waiter/waitress
Work with a computer: editor, secretary, cashier
Stand at work: salesperson, janitor, police officer, doctor, nurse, baker, waiter/waitress, cashier
Sit at work: editor, secretary, receptionist, security guard

9 What are you having for breakfast?

Topic/function: Breakfast foods; talking about eating habits

Structure: Adverbs of frequency

Summary

This documentary sequence opens with shots of a variety of typical breakfast foods eaten in the United States and Canada. A reporter, Neil Murray, is eating in a restaurant that specializes in breakfast. He describes what he is eating and drinking, and then interviews several other people about what they are having for breakfast.

Cultural note

Many people in the United States and Canada tend to place a great deal of importance on having a good breakfast to start their day. Although there are some people who have nothing more than a cup of coffee and possibly a donut for breakfast, almost everyone would agree that this is not a healthy habit.

 *Preview*

1 VOCABULARY Breakfast

In these activities, students are introduced to vocabulary related to the types of breakfast foods and beverages presented in the sequence.

A Books closed. As a warm-up to the activity, ask, "With what meal do people drink their first cup of coffee of the day?" Elicit or provide the word *breakfast*. Ask students to call out the names of any breakfast foods and drinks that they might know; if you wish, write on the board any words that students offer.

■ Books open. Have students look at the items in the picture. Use the example to explain the task. Then read through the list of foods and drinks. Have students repeat each description after you with correct stress and pronunciation. (Note: This would be a good time to teach students how to identify which syllables are stressed. Tell

students to listen for the loudest syllables when you say each word or phrase. For number 2, for example, say, "A **ba**gel with **cream** cheese," as you tap a pencil on the desk to emphasize the stressed syllables. Write the phrase on the board, and mark the stressed syllables. Repeat the process with some of the other words and phrases.)

■ Have students work individually to match the breakfast foods with their correct descriptions. Circulate to offer help and encouragement.

■ Put students into pairs to compare answers. Then check answers around the class by calling on volunteers to say an answer and write it on the board.

Answers

1) l	6) b	11) n
2) a	7) h	12) j
3) o	8) g	13) m
4) d	9) f	14) e
5) k	10) i	15) c

B *Group work* Books open. Explain the task, and go over the model conversation. Then quickly check that students understand the meanings of *usually*, *always*, and *never*.

■ Put students into groups of four to take turns asking and answering questions about their favorite breakfast foods. Circulate to help with stress and pronunciation.

■ Call on volunteer groups to share their information with the rest of the class.

2 WHAT DO YOU SEE?

In this activity, students prepare to watch the sequence by using visual information to identify some of the breakfast foods that people are eating in the video.

■ Books open. Explain the task, and lead students through the list of foods. Answer any questions about vocabulary as they arise. Tell students that they will see foods in the video that are not included in the list. Also point out that you will play the sequence more than once if necessary.

■ Play the entire sequence with the sound off, starting from the appearance of the woman eating the bagel. Have students watch and work alone to check (✓) the correct answers. Replay the video sequence to let students check their own answers.

■ Put students into pairs to compare answers. Then go over the answers around the class.

Answers
a bagel with cream cheese and tea
a bowl of fruit
French toast, bacon, and coffee
pancakes with sausages
fried eggs with toast
cereal with juice and hot chocolate
yogurt and an English muffin
an omelette

 Watch the video

3 GET THE PICTURE

In this activity, students watch and listen to find out the main foods that five of the restaurant customers are having for breakfast.

■ Books open. Have students look at the photos as you read through the list of foods. Point out that only the main courses are listed. Also explain that some of the people may have more than one food checked.

■ Play the entire sequence with the sound on. Have students complete the task while they watch.

■ Check if anyone needs to watch the sequence again to complete the task; replay as needed. Then put students into pairs to compare their answers before going over the answers around the class.

Answers
1) a bagel
2) French toast
3) pancakes
4) cereal
5) an English muffin, yogurt

4 WATCH FOR DETAILS

In this activity, students watch and listen more closely in order to identify details about the restaurant customers' breakfasts.

■ Books open. Explain the task, and go over the example. Have students, working individually, read through the lists and check (✓) any answers they can before watching the sequence. Then have students compare predictions around the class.

■ Play the sequence, and have students check the predictions they made and complete the activity as they watch and listen. While students work, write the following on the board for them to use when comparing answers:

A: In picture 1, the reporter is having

‾‾‾‾‾‾‾‾‾‾‾ .
He isn't having ‾‾‾‾‾‾‾‾ .

B: Yes, that's right./No, that's not right.
He's having ‾‾‾‾‾‾‾‾ .

■ When everyone has completed the task, model the sample language that you wrote on the board. As pairs compare answers, circulate and check for accuracy. Replay the sequence as necessary before going over the answers with the class.

Answers
1) scrambled eggs, bacon, toast, coffee, orange juice
2) a bagel with cream cheese, tea with lemon
3) grapes, watermelon, bananas, honeydew melon, coffee
4) pancakes, bananas, blueberries, coffee with cream
5) fried eggs, toast, coffee

Optional activity

- Books closed. Write the following sentences on the board:

1) The first woman _____ has tea with lemon.
2) The second woman _____ has fruit for breakfast.
3) The first man _____ has eggs for breakfast.
4) The second man _____ has French toast for breakfast.
5) The third woman _____ has bacon for breakfast.

- Tell students that they are going to watch the sequence again and that they should listen for and write down the missing adverb of frequency in each of the sentences on the board.

- Play the sequence, stopping after each person mentioned in the statements on the board. Ask volunteers to give the correct answer and to fill in the blank on the board. Then check answers around the class. (5–10 minutes)

Answers

1) always   4) sometimes
2) always   5) (very) seldom/rarely
3) seldom

Follow-up

5 WHAT'S YOUR OPINION?

In this extension activity, students say whether or not they like some of the breakfast foods shown in the video.

- *Pair work* Books open. Explain the task, and ask volunteers to describe the breakfast foods shown in the photos. Then go over the sample dialog, having students repeat after you with correct stress and intonation.

- Put students into pairs to talk about the breakfasts. As students share opinions, circulate to offer help and encouragement.

- Have selected pairs share their opinions with the rest of the class.

Possible answers (from left to right)

A: I like this breakfast. I love bananas and yogurt.
B: Really? I don't like bananas. But I like English muffins.

A: I don't like this breakfast. I hate cold cereal.
B: Really? I like cold cereal. And I love apple juice.

A: I love this breakfast. I love fruit.
B: I love fruit, too.

A: I hate this breakfast. I don't like pancakes.
B: Really? I love pancakes.

A: I like this breakfast. I like omelettes. And I love toast.
B: Me, too.

6 PLAN A MENU

In this communicative activity, students use the language presented in the sequence to plan their own breakfast menus.

- *Pair work* Books closed. Ask students if they know of any restaurants that serve mainly, or only, breakfast foods. Point out that some restaurants in the United States and Canada specialize in breakfast. If necessary, explain that here, the word *serve* means "to give someone food and drinks as part of a meal."

- Books open. Tell students to look at the picture of the menu. Ask the following questions, and have students call out the answers:

What's the name of this restaurant? (It's called Happy Egg Restaurant.)
When is it open? (It's open 24 hours a day, 7 days a week.)

- Explain the task, and go over the model dialog. Put students into pairs to plan their ten breakfast dishes as well as drinks to accompany them. Circulate to help with vocabulary.

- If time allows, join pairs together to compare menus in small groups. Then have selected students share their menus with the class.

Optional activity

- *Group work* Books closed. Tell students that they are going to open a new restaurant. Have Exercise 6 pairs join together to make groups of four. Tell groups to combine their menus and to decide on a suitable name for their restaurant. Then have students attach a price in the local currency to each of their meals.

- Have groups take turns telling their classmates about their restaurant. (10 minutes)

Language close-up

7 WHAT DID THEY SAY?

This cloze activity develops bottom-up listening skills by having students complete the interview between Neil Murray and the first two restaurant customers.

■ Books open. Tell students to look at the photos. Ask if anyone remembers what the interviewer is having for breakfast (scrambled eggs, bacon, toast, coffee, and orange juice). Then tell students to read silently through the conversations and, working individually or in pairs, to fill in any blanks they can before watching the sequence.

■ Play this segment as many times as necessary while students work alone to check their predictions and complete the task. Then have students compare answers with a partner.

■ Go over the answers with the class. Then replay the segment as students follow along in their books and check their work.

■ Model the conversations or, if you wish, lead a choral repetition of them. Then put students into groups of three to practice the conversations, encouraging them to use the "Look Up and Say" technique. Finally, have one or two selected groups act out the conversations in front of the class.

Answers

1) Neil: Good **morning**. What are you **having** for breakfast?
   Woman 1: I'm having a **bagel** with cream **cheese** and hot tea with **lemon**.
   Neil: Do you **always** have tea for breakfast?
   Woman 1: Yes, I have hot tea with **lemon** all **day** long.

2) Neil: Good morning.
   Woman 2: Well, good morning.
   Neil: **What** are you having for breakfast?
   Woman 2: I'm **starting** out with a bowl of **fruit**. I **like** to begin my **day** with a **good** breakfast.
   Neil: What **fruit** do you have in your bowl?
   Woman 2: This morning, I have **grapes**, watermelon, **bananas**, and honeydew melon.

Neil: Do you **always** have **fruit** for breakfast?
Woman 2: Yes.
Neil: What **else** are you having?
Woman 2: This **morning**, I will have **bacon** and **eggs** and toast.

Optional activity

■ **Pair work** Books open. Put students into pairs, and tell them to rewrite the second conversation with their own choice of breakfast foods. Tell students they can change as much or as little as they want. Circulate to help and to check for accuracy.

■ Ask selected pairs to act out their new conversations for the rest of the class. Through a show of hands, take a poll on who had the best breakfast. (10–15 minutes)

8 ADVERBS OF FREQUENCY
Talking about eating habits

In these activities, students practice with adverbs of frequency, the grammatical focus of this sequence.

A Books open. Tell students to look at the picture. Ask volunteers to say what they think the woman is eating for breakfast. Ask, "What do you think of this meal? Is it large, small, good, healthy?" Have students call out their answers.

■ Explain the task, and go over the adverbs of frequency in the box, using them in example sentences as necessary. Point out that students should complete the six sentences with adverbs that truthfully describe their own situations.

■ Have students work alone to fill in the blanks and then compare answers with a partner.

■ Check answers around the class, and accept all answers that make sense.

B **Class activity** Books open. Explain the task. Point out the use of *but* to express contrast in the sample sentence.

■ Have students write a sentence based on their discussion with their partner in part A. Then have students take turns sharing their sentences with the class.

10 What sports do you play?

Topic/functions: Sports; talking about abilities and interests

Structure: *Can* for ability

Summary

This sequence starts out with a series of shots of people exercising and playing several different sports at the Chelsea Piers Sports and Entertainment Center in New York City. Mary Purdy, a reporter, is standing in front of the complex. She lists a few of the many sports that people can do there. She then interviews people who are Rollerblading, rock climbing, ice-skating, and hitting golf balls.

 *Preview*

1 VOCABULARY Sports

These activities prepare students for working with the language presented in the sequence by introducing the vocabulary for various sports.

A Books closed. As a warm-up to the activity, ask the class, "What's your favorite sport?" As students call out their answers, write them on the board. Supply vocabulary as needed.

■ Books open. Explain the task. Then model the names of the sports in the box, having students repeat after you with correct pronunciation.

■ Ask students to look at the pictures, and then have them work individually to match the words and the pictures.

■ Put students into pairs to compare answers. Then go over the answers with the class.

Answers

1) ice-skating	5) baseball
2) volleyball	6) rock climbing
3) gymnastics	7) soccer
4) golf	8) Rollerblading

B Books closed. Ask a selected student, "Can you ice-skate?" Write the question and the answer on the board. Ask another student, "Can you do

gymnastics?" and add the question and the answer to the board. Continue with this process until you have both an affirmative and a negative answer on the board for each question.

■ *Pair work* Books open. Call attention to the language box containing the three patterns commonly used when talking about sports and exercise. You may want to point out the following for each pattern, noting that there are almost always exceptions to grammar "rules":

Can you play . . . ? is usually used with games, specifically ball games.
Can you do . . . ? is used with exercise-type activities.
Can you . . . ? is used with individual – rather than team – sports.

Ask volunteers to suggest other sports for each of the three patterns.

Possible answers

Can you play . . . ?	*Can you . . . ?*
basketball	jog
football	ski
tennis	swim
Can you do . . . ?	
aerobics	
yoga	

■ Explain the task, and model the sample conversation. Have students repeat after you with the correct stress and intonation.

■ Put students into pairs to take turns asking and answering questions about each other's sporting abilities and talents. Circulate to offer help and to check for accuracy.

Optional activity

■ *Group work* Books open. Put students into groups of four or five. Have each group write on slips of paper the names of all the sports in Exercise 1. Then have them fold the papers and drop them into a container such as a bag or a box. Each group should have their own container.

(procedure continues on next page)

■ Tell students to take turns picking a slip of paper out of the container, looking at it without letting anyone else see it, and then pantomiming the sport on the paper. The other group members guess the sport being acted out. (10–15 minutes)

2 *WHAT DO YOU SEE?*

In this activity, students prepare to watch the sequence by identifying some of the sports that they will see in the video.

■ Books open. Explain the task, and lead students through the list of sports. You may want to point out that in this list *football* refers to American football and not to soccer.

■ Before playing the video, explain that students will see many sports that are not listed and that the shots of sports change very quickly. Play the first minute of the video sequence with the sound off (until the reporter appears). Then have students try to remember and check (✓) the sports that they saw.

■ Replay the sequence for students to check their answers. You may need to pause the video several times to give students a chance to refer to the list.

■ Put students into pairs to compare answers. Then go over the answers with the class.

Answers
basketball
ice-skating
Rollerblading
gymnastics
golf

 Watch the video

3 *GET THE PICTURE*

In this activity, students watch and listen to the entire sequence to find out what sports the people who are interviewed play.

■ Books open. Explain the task, and have students look carefully at the photos of the people from the sequence.

■ Play the entire sequence. Tell students, as they watch, to check (✓) the sport(s) each person plays.

■ Have students compare answers with a partner

or in small groups.

■ Ask if anyone needs to watch the sequence again, and replay as necessary.

■ Go over the answers with the class.

Answers
1) Rollerblading
2) golf, Rollerblading
3) rock climbing
4) ice-skating, rock climbing
5) ice-skating
6) golf

4 *WATCH FOR DETAILS*

In this activity, students focus more closely on language by watching and listening in order to identify the questions that the interviewer asks and to determine how the people answer those questions.

■ Books open. Explain the task, and lead students through the questions and responses. Answer any vocabulary questions that students might have. Then have students work individually to predict the answers before viewing.

■ Play the sequence, and have students check and revise their predictions as they view.

■ Put students into pairs to compare answers before you go over them with the class.

Answers
1) Can you ice-skate?
   No.
2) Is this your first time Rollerblading?
   Yes.
3) Is this a fun sport?
   Yes.
4) How often do you come here?
   Every Friday.
5) Are you a good skater?
   No.
6) How do you like this place?
   It's fantastic!

Optional activity

■ Books closed. Put the following questions on the board:

1) Is the first woman alone?
2) What's the first man's favorite sport, Rollerblading or golf?
3) Can rock climbing be dangerous?
4) What's the children's favorite sport?
5) How often does the man in picture 5 go skating?
6) How often does the man in picture 6 play golf?

■ Tell students to watch the sequence again, this time listening for the answers to the questions on the board. Tell students to raise their hands when they hear the answers. Pause the video, and have students call out their answers. (5–10 minutes)

Answers

1) No, she isn't. (She's with her sister-in-law.)
2) The man's favorite sport is golf.
3) Yes, at times.
4) The children's favorite sport is ice-skating.
5) He goes skating two or three times a week.
6) He plays golf every week.

Follow-up

5 ROLE PLAY *A day at the sports center*

In this extension activity, students have the chance to be creative by taking turns playing the roles of a reporter and someone taking part in one or more sports at the Chelsea Piers Sports and Entertainment Center.

■ *Pair work* Books open. Have students look at each of the photos of people participating in sports at the sports center. Describe the task, and go over the sample language in the box. Then tell students to take turns playing speaker B, someone taking part in one or more activities at the sports center. (If you wish, take the role of speaker B and model the activity with a student.)

■ Put students into pairs to take turns role-playing the reporter and a visitor to the sports center. As students work, circulate to help and to check for accuracy.

■ If you wish, ask several pairs to act out their role plays for the class.

6 FIND SOMEONE WHO...

This communicative activity further develops students' understanding as they find out about their classmates' sports abilities and interests.

■ *Class activity* Books open. Explain the task, and lead students through the eight phrases in the chart. If you feel it necessary, model the activity for the class by asking the first question – "Do you play a sport every week?" – and asking students to raise their hands if their answer is "Yes." Write those students' names on the board.

■ Have students stand and move around the room, asking their classmates questions in order to come up with one name for each of the categories in the chart. Encourage students to talk to as many classmates as possible. (Note: Because some students will resort to pointing to their form or simply repeating the given phrase, it is a good idea to circulate to encourage students to form questions.)

■ Have students share their information about their classmates by making statements from their charts for the class. Continue until a statement has been made about each student.

Optional activity

■ *Group work* Books open. Put students into groups of between eight and ten to take a class survey. Tell them to use their chart in Exercise 6 to find out how many students fit each item. Have each group assign a secretary to keep track of the numbers while different students ask their group members the questions.

■ Have each group report the results of their survey by making statements such as, "Nine students in our group play a sport every week." Keep a tally of all the groups' answers on the board. (5–10 minutes)

 **Language close-up**

7 WHAT DID THEY SAY?

This cloze activity has students focus on specific language used by Mary Purdy and the first woman that she interviews.

▪ Books open. Read the instructions, and tell students to look at the photos. Ask students if they remember the name of the reporter (Mary) and what the first person interviewed is doing (Rollerblading).

▪ Have students, working individually or in pairs, read through the interview and fill in any blanks they can before watching the sequence. Then have students compare predictions around the class.

▪ Play this segment of the sequence through once, and have students work alone to check their predictions and complete the task.

▪ Before going over the answers with the class, have students compare answers with a partner. Then replay the segment as needed.

▪ Model the conversation or, if you wish, lead a choral repetition of it. Then put students into pairs to practice the conversation. Finally, have one or two selected pairs act out the conversation in front of the class, using the "Look Up and Say" technique.

Answers

Mary: Hi! This is Mary Purdy, and **today** I'm in New York City at the Chelsea Piers Sports and Entertainment Center. There are a lot of **different** kinds of **things** to do here. You can play soccer or **basketball**. You can **go** ice-skating **or** Rollerblading. You can practice your swing. You can do **gymnastics**. You can **swim** or lift weights. You can even go **rock** climbing. Let's go **talk** to some of the people who are here today. Come on!

Woman: Hi.

Mary: Hi. So what are you **doing** here **today**?

Woman: I'm **here** with my **sister**-in-law.

Mary: And **right** now you're Rollerblading?

Woman: Yes, I **am**.

Mary: **Can** you ice-**skate**?

Woman: **No**.

Mary: But **you** can Rollerblade.

Woman: Yes, I **can**.

Optional activity

▪ *Pair work* Books open. Put students into pairs and tell them to rewrite the dialog, changing Rollerblading to a sport of their own choice. Circulate to help and to check for accuracy.

▪ Have pairs read or act out their new conversations for the class. (10–15 minutes)

8 TALKING ABOUT ABILITIES AND INTERESTS

In these activities, students extend and personalize the information in the sequence by asking and answering questions about their own sports-related abilities and interests.

A Books open. Have students look at the illustration. Ask students, "What are these people doing?" (They're skiing.) Then ask, "Can the man ski?" (No, he can't.) Have students call out their answers.

▪ Explain the task, and go over the short answers in the box. Have students work individually to write their answers. Circulate to help and to check for accuracy.

Answers

1) Yes, I can./No, I can't.   4) Yes, I do./No, I don't.
2) Yes, I do./No, I don't.   5) Yes, I do./No, I don't.
3) Yes, I can./No, I can't.   6) Yes, I can./No, I can't.

B Books open. Explain the task, and tell students to work alone to write their five questions on a separate sheet of paper. Again, you may wish to circulate to offer help and encouragement.

▪ Put students into pairs to take turns asking and answering questions about their own sporting abilities and interests. Finally, ask several pairs to share their questions and answers with the rest of the class.

11 A weekend in New York City

Topic/function: Sight-seeing activities; talking about plans	
Structure: Future with *be going to*	

Summary

This sequence opens with several shots of popular New York City sight-seeing destinations. Chuck Santoro, a reporter, then interviews several people about what they plan to do during their visit to New York City.

Cultural note

Visitors from all over the world can be found on the streets of New York City at almost any time of the year. Some of the most popular sight-seeing destinations include the Statue of Liberty, Central Park, and the Empire State Building.

 **Preview**

1 *VOCABULARY* Sight-seeing activities

This exercise introduces the vocabulary for the New York City sight-seeing activities that students will see and hear about in the video.

A Books closed. Ask, "Where do visitors in our city (or town) go?" Have students call out their answers.

■ Books open. For each photo, ask students, "What do you see in this picture?" Do not have students name the scene, but rather have them describe it with sentences such as, "I see some theater signs."

■ Explain the task, and lead students through the list of activities in the box; if you wish, have students repeat after you with correct stress and pronunciation. (Note: These phrases are particularly useful for stress practice. Have students mark the stressed syllables in these phrases and then read them aloud again.)

■ Have students work alone to match the activities with the appropriate pictures. Circulate to offer help and encouragement.

■ After students compare answers in pairs, go over the answers with the class.

Answers
1) c	5) g
2) h	6) b
3) f	7) e
4) a	8) d

B *Group work* Books open. Explain the task, and go over the model dialog. Then tell students to look back at the pictures in part A and to choose the activity that seems the most interesting to them.

■ Put students into groups of three or four to take turns asking and answering questions about one another's sight-seeing choices. Circulate to help and to check for accuracy.

2 *WHAT DO YOU SEE?*

In this activity, students prepare to watch the video by using visual information to identify the activities that appear in the sequence.

■ Books open. Explain the task, and ask volunteers each to read aloud an activity on the list. Explain that students will see some places or activities that are not listed.

■ Play the entire sequence with the sound off. As students watch, have them check (✓) their answers. Then put the students into pairs to compare answers before going over the answers with the class. (Note: Tell students not to worry if they didn't get all the answers correct. They'll have a chance to correct their answers when they watch the video with the sound on, in the next activity.)

Answers
take a walk in Central Park
take a bus tour
visit the Empire State Building
take a carriage ride
see a Broadway show

Watch the video

3 *GET THE PICTURE*

In this activity, students watch and listen in order to find out one specific piece of information about each person or group of people interviewed: where they're from.

■ Books open. Explain the task, and read through the list of places with the class. You may wish to point out that Georgia is in the southeastern part of the U.S., Texas is in the southwestern part of the U.S., and New Jersey is right next to New York. If necessary, also explain that Puerto Rico is an island in the Caribbean, off the southeastern coast of the U.S., and that Ireland is an island in Europe, in the British Isles.

■ Play the entire sequence with the sound on. Have students watch and check (✓) the correct answers as they view.

■ Have students compare answers with a partner. Then play the sequence again if necessary.

■ Go over the answers with the class by asking selected students to call out answers.

Answers
1) Puerto Rico
2) New Jersey
3) Ireland
4) Texas
5) New York
6) Georgia

4 *WATCH FOR DETAILS*

In this activity, students focus more closely on details by watching and listening for specific information about what the people interviewed plan to do while they're in New York City.

■ Books open. Explain the task, and lead students through the phrases under the six photos. If you wish, have students predict answers before they watch the sequence.

■ Play the entire sequence with the sound on as students work alone to complete the task.

■ Have students compare answers with a partner. Then ask if anyone needs to watch the sequence again. Replay as necessary, and then check answers around the class.

Answers
1) visit different places, see a musical, go out for dinner
2) take a carriage ride
3) visit Central Park, go skating, go to the zoo
4) go to Central Park, go to the Statue of Liberty, see a show
5) take a walk, run
6) take a bus tour, see the Statue of Liberty, visit the Empire State Building

5 *WHAT THE PEOPLE SAY*

In this activity, students focus more closely on language by watching and listening to determine what three of the people say in the video.

■ Books open. Explain the task. Then have students read the incomplete sentences silently and predict the missing words before viewing.

■ Play the sequence, and have students check and revise their predictions as they view. (Note: You may want to pause the video after each relevant scene to give students enough time to write their answers.)

■ Put students into pairs to compare answers before going over them with the class.

Answers
1) every weekend
2) sixteenth birthday
3) watch all the people

Follow-up

La *Language close-up*

6 A DAY IN NEW YORK

In these activities, students discuss the things in New York City that they find interesting. They use the information that they have learned about the city to plan a day there. (Note: Since students will be working in small groups, they may need to negotiate and compromise as they make their plans.)

A Books open. Lead students through the photos, and call on a different volunteer to read each caption aloud.

▪ *Group work* Explain the task, and then put students into groups of three or four. Tell each group to choose a secretary, who will write down the group's plans and share them with the class in part B of the exercise.

▪ Tell students that their group must decide where to visit and what to do: two things in the morning, two things in the afternoon, and one thing in the evening. Put the following phrases on the board for students to use while making their plans:
How about verb + -ing _____ ?
Let's _____ .

▪ As the groups work on their plans, circulate to offer help and encouragement.

B *Class activity* Books open. Explain the task, and go over the model language.

▪ After all the group secretaries share their groups' plans with the class, have students vote on the most interesting day.

Possible answers
In the morning, we're going to shop on Fifth Avenue and visit the United Nations. In the afternoon, we're going to take a ride on the subway and go skating in Central Park. In the evening, we're going to see a movie in Times Square.

In the morning, we're going to take a ride on the subway and go skating in Central Park. In the afternoon, we're going to visit the United Nations and see a movie in Times Square. In the evening, we're going to eat in a restaurant in Chinatown.

7 WHAT DID THEY SAY?

This cloze activity develops bottom-up listening skills by having students complete the interview between the reporter and the couple from Puerto Rico.

▪ Books open. Tell students to look at the photos, and ask if they remember the name of the reporter (Chuck) and where the couple is from (Puerto Rico).

▪ Have students, working individually or in pairs, read through the interview and fill in any blanks they can before watching the sequence.

▪ Play this segment of the sequence as many times as necessary while students work alone to check their predictions and complete the task. Then have students compare answers with a partner.

▪ Go over the answers with the class. Then replay the segment as students follow along in their books and check their work.

▪ Model the conversation or, if you wish, lead a choral repetition of it. Then have students practice the conversation in groups of three.

Answers

Chuck: New York City! People **come** here from all over the **country** – and all over the **world**. Let's **talk** to some of them. . . . **Excuse** me.
Man: Yes?
Chuck: Where are you **two** from?
Man: Puerto Rico.
Chuck: Puerto Rico! And **what** are you going to **do** while you're **here** in New York?
Man: Visit . . . uh . . . visit **different** places.
Chuck: Uh, **where** are you going to **go**?
Woman: Go to **see** *Beauty and the Beast*.
Chuck: *Beauty and the Beast* . . . the **musical**.
Woman: Yes.
Chuck: Well, are you going to **do** anything **tonight**?
Man: **Dinner**.
Chuck: Are you **enjoying** your trip?
Man: **Very** much so, yeah.

(see next page for an optional activity)

Optional activity

▪ **Group work** Books open. Put students into groups of three, and tell them to role-play the situation of being interviewed by a local person about their plans. Tell them to choose one group member to be the reporter. Explain that the other two are to role-play being visitors to your city.

▪ Have groups practice their role plays. Then ask several groups to perform their role plays for the class. (15 minutes)

8 FUTURE WITH BE GOING TO
Talking about plans

In these activities, students practice talking about plans (the functional focus of the sequence) using the future with *be going to* (the grammatical focus of the sequence).

A Books open. As students look at the picture, ask, "What's the woman going to do?" When a student answers correctly (She's going to see a movie. OR She's going to go to the movies.), write the sentence on the board.

▪ Explain the task, and model the example.

▪ Have students work alone to complete the task and then compare answers with a partner as you circulate to check for accuracy.

▪ Go over the answers with the class.

Answers
1) A: **Are** you **going to do** anything on Friday night?
   B: Yes, I'**m going to see** a movie.
2) A: What time **are** you **going to leave** school today?
   B: I'**m going to go** home at 7:00 P.M.
3) A: What **are** you **going to have** for dinner tonight?
   B: I think I'**m going to have** fish.
4) A: **Are** you **going to study** English tonight?
   B: No, I'**m going to watch** TV.

B **Pair work** Books open. Explain the task, and put students into pairs.

▪ As students take turns asking and answering the questions in part A with their own information, circulate to help.

▪ Ask several pairs each to share a question-and-answer set with the class.

Optional activity

▪ **Group work** Books closed. Ask students to call out the names of cities that they would like to visit. Form groups with students who have the same or similar city or region choices.

▪ Have students plan a trip to the area that they chose. Tell them to choose five sight-seeing destinations and then to write a description of their plans. Encourage the use of the future with *be going to* in students' descriptions.

▪ Have groups read their descriptions to the class. If time allows, encourage students to ask questions to get more information. (10 minutes)

12 The doctor and the patient

| Topic/function: | Health problems; talking about health problems |
| Structure: | Imperatives |

Summary

The sequence opens in the waiting room of a doctor's office. After the receptionist tells one of the patients, Mr. Lewis, that the doctor is ready to see him, the scene changes to show the doctor. Dr. North is clearly in pain with what seems to be a backache. Dr. North examines Mr. Lewis and gives him medication and advice that will cure his earache. Then, as Mr. Lewis is getting ready to leave, he notices Dr. North's discomfort. The doctor/patient roles are reversed as Mr. Lewis solves Dr. North's health problem.

 Preview

1 VOCABULARY Actions

These activities prepare students for working with the language presented in the sequence by introducing the vocabulary for various types of actions.

A Books closed. As a warm-up to the activity, point to your knees and ask, "What are these?" Have students call out the answer while you write it on the board. Repeat the procedure with your feet. Then check for students' understanding of *left* and *right* by telling them first to raise their left hand and then their right.

■ Books open. Explain the task. Then model the sentences in the box, having the class repeat after you with correct stress and pronunciation.

■ After giving students a minute or so to look over the illustrations, have them work individually to write the sentences under the correct pictures.

■ Put students into pairs to compare answers. Then go over the answers with the class.

Answers
1) Bring your right knee up.
2) Sit down.
3) Lie down.
4) Bend your knees.
5) Bring your left knee up.

B *Pair work* Books open. Explain the task. Then put students into pairs to take turns calling out and doing the actions in part A.

■ As students work, circulate to offer help and encouragement. If time allows, ask several pairs to "perform" in front of the class.

Optional activity

■ *Class activity* Books closed. Tell students that they are going to play a game called "Simon Says." Then explain the rules of the game: Students will all stand up. You will give a series of commands – one at a time, with most of them starting with the phrase "Simon says." If students hear the phrase, they must obey the command; if the command doesn't start with "Simon says," they shouldn't do anything. Tell students that if they do an action without hearing "Simon says" or if they do the wrong action, they're out and they have to sit down. The last student standing is the winner and gets to lead the next game. (Possible actions: Sit down. Stand up. Smile. Laugh. Bend your knees. Touch your knees. Touch your toes. Close your eyes. Say your name. Touch your nose.) (5–10 minutes)

■ Before starting the game, give this example:

Simon says touch your toes. (*Students touch their toes.*) Touch your toes. (*Students do nothing.*)

2 WHAT DO YOU SEE?

In this activity, students prepare to watch the sequence by using visual information to make predictions about the story.

■ Books open. Have students look at the photos of the doctor and the patient. As a warm-up to the activity, ask individual students, "Do you go to the doctor often? What's your doctor's name?"

(procedure continues on next page)

■ Explain the task. Then lead students through the three questions, answering any questions about vocabulary or content as they arise.

■ Put students into pairs to look at the photos and to guess the answers to the three questions. Then ask selected students to report their predictions to the class. Accept all answers at this point.

■ Tell students they will watch the sequence without the sound and they should check their predictions against what they see.

■ Play the entire sequence with the sound off as students watch and check their predictions.

■ Tell students that they will find out if their answers are correct in the next activity.

Watch the video

3 GET THE PICTURE

In the first activity, students watch and listen to check the predictions they made in Exercise 2. In the second activity, they watch and listen for the information needed to complete the doctor's notes about the patient.

A Books open. Explain the task, and make sure that students turn to Exercise 2 on page 46 to check their predictions as they watch the sequence.

■ Play the sequence with the sound on as students complete the task. Then have selected students provide the answers, and replay the sequence as necessary.

Answers
1) The patient
2) The doctor
3) The doctor

B Books open. Explain the task, and review the information on the patient chart and prescription pad, making sure students understand the sample completion under *Patient's name* on the chart.

■ Books closed. Play the entire sequence with the sound on. Tell students to watch and listen for the information that the patient gives the doctor about his ailment and for the advice and instructions that the doctor gives in response.

■ Books open. Have students work alone to fill in the missing information. Then have students compare answers in pairs or small groups.

■ Ask if anyone needs to watch the sequence again, and replay if necessary before going over the answers with the class. To go over the answers, write on the board the patient chart and the prescription notes as they appear in the book. Call on volunteers to come up to the board to fill in the missing information.

Answers

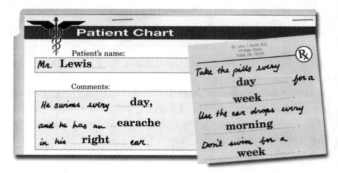

4 WATCH FOR DETAILS

In this activity, students watch and listen for specific information about what happens in the second half of the sequence – when the patient helps the doctor with his backache.

■ Books open. To prepare for the activity, put students into pairs to look at the photos and to say what is happening in each one. Circulate to help with vocabulary. (Note: At this point, students should have enough language to discuss what they see in pictures.) Have selected students share their descriptions with the class.

■ Explain the task. Read through the items, answering any questions about vocabulary.

■ Books closed. Play the sequence with the sound on. Remind students to watch and listen for information that will help them answer the questions.

■ Books open. Have students, working individually or in pairs, answer the questions and then compare answers with a partner.

■ Check answers around the class. If there are errors, replay the sequence so that students can check and correct their answers.

Answers
1) His father often has a backache.
2) Sit down.
3) The right knee.
4) The receptionist.
5) The patient.
6) Fine.

Follow-up

5 HEALTH PROBLEMS

In these communicative activities, students first match statements to pictures, then they use the pictures to role-play a conversation between Dr. North and Mr. Lewis, and finally they talk about their own health.

A Books open. Have students look at the four photos. Have volunteers each read aloud one of the sentences to the rest of the class.

■ Have students work alone to match the sentences with the photos. After students compare answers in pairs, check answers around the class.

Answers
1) Lie down on the table.
2) Bend your knees.
3) Bring your right knee up.
4) Bring your left knee up.

B *Pair work* Books open. Explain the task, and go over the model beginning to the conversation between the doctor and the patient. If you wish, have students repeat after you with correct stress and intonation.

■ Put students into pairs to take turns playing the roles of Dr. North and Mr. Lewis. As they work, circulate to offer help and encouragement, and to check for accuracy.

■ After a few minutes, have selected pairs perform their role plays for the rest of the class.

Possible answer
Mr. Lewis: First, sit down. How's that?
Dr. North: Much better. Oh, thank you.
Mr. Lewis: Now lie down on the table.
Dr. North: OK.
Mr. Lewis: Now bend your knees and put your feet up on the table.
Dr. North: Like this?

Mr. Lewis: Yes, that's right. Now bring your right knee up to your chest. And now your left knee. Very good.

C *Pair work* Books open. Have students look at the illustrations, and make sure they can pronounce the name of each ailment pictured.

■ Explain the task. Then go over the language in the sample dialog, pointing out the use of *ever* in the question. If necessary, put the following adverbs of frequency on the board to help students in their conversations: *always, often, sometimes, seldom, never.*

■ Put students into pairs to take turns asking and answering questions about their health. Circulate to check for accuracy.

■ After several pairs share one or two of their conversations with the rest of the class, take a poll to find out if there is anyone in the class who never gets sick.

Optional activity

■ *Group work* Books open or closed. Put students into groups to think of more reasons to go to the doctor. Tell students to assign the job of secretary to one of their group members. As groups brainstorm, circulate to help with vocabulary questions.

■ After a few minutes, have group secretaries each report on their group's ideas. You may want to write the better ideas on the board and tell students to copy the words or phrases into their notebooks. (5–10 minutes)

Possible answers

a backache	a cough	a sore throat
a headache	sore eyes	sore muscles

Language close-up

6 WHAT DID THEY SAY?

This cloze activity has students focus on specific language used in the opening segment of the sequence.

■ Books open. Read the instructions, and tell students to look at the photos. Ask students if they remember the patient's name (Mr. Lewis);

(procedure continues on next page)

then ask, "Who is the woman standing at the door?" (The receptionist.)

■ Have students, working individually or in pairs, read through the conversation and fill in any blanks they can before watching the sequence. Then students compare predictions around the class.

■ Play this segment of the sequence through once, and have students work alone to check their predictions and complete the task.

■ Before going over the answers with the class, have students compare answers with a partner. Then replay the segment as needed.

■ Model the conversation or, if you wish, lead a choral or an individual repetition of it. Then put students into groups of three to practice the conversation. Have groups practice three times so that each student has a chance to play each of the three characters. Finally, have one or two groups act out the conversation in front of the class.

Answers

Receptionist: Mr. Lewis?
Mr. Lewis: Yes?
Receptionist: The **doctor** will **see** you now.
Doctor: **Come** in. Mr. Lewis. **How** are you?
Mr. Lewis: **Fine**, thanks.
Doctor: What's the **problem** today?
Mr. Lewis: It's my **ear**. I have an **earache**.
Doctor: Well, let's have a **look**. Please **sit** down over **here**. Is it the **right** ear or the **left**?
Mr. Lewis: It's the **right** one.
Doctor: **OK** now. Let's see. Mmm. Yes. . . . Yep. Do you **swim**, Mr. Lewis?
Mr. Lewis: Yes, I do. I **swim** every **morning**.
Doctor: Well, I'm going to **give** you these ear drops . . . and some **pills**.
Mr. Lewis: Thanks, **Doctor**.

Optional activity

■ *Group work* Books open. Have students work in groups of three to write a possible conversation involving the receptionist, the doctor, and the patient that comes in after Mr. Lewis. As students work on their new conversations, circulate to help.

■ Have groups read or act out their new conversations for the class. (10–15 minutes)

7 IMPERATIVES *Giving advice*

In these extension activities, students work with affirmative and negative imperatives to give advice on home remedies for health problems.

A Books open. Have students look at the illustration. Ask, "What's this man's problem? What does he say?" Call on a volunteer for the answer. (I have a sore throat.) Then ask, "What's his friend's advice?" (Drink hot tea with lemon.)

■ Explain the task, and lead students through the advice in the box and each of the health complaints. Answer any relevant questions.

■ Have students work alone to write a piece of advice that completes each of the conversations. Circulate to offer help and encouragement.

■ Put students into pairs to compare answers. Then check answers around the class by having selected pairs read the completed conversations.

Answers

1) Drink hot tea with lemon.
2) Take two aspirin and close your eyes.
3) Don't lift heavy things.
4) Stay in bed for two days.
5) Don't try new foods.
6) Drink a lot of orange juice.

B Books open. Explain the task, and give students five minutes to write their own advice for each of the problems in part A. Then have students form small groups to compare answers.

■ Ask students to call out their advice for each problem, and create a class list on the board of remedies and advice for solving the six health problems in the activity.

Optional activity

■ *Pair work* Books open or closed. Tell students to take turns role-playing a doctor/patient situation. Have one student be the patient and tell the doctor what is wrong; the other student plays the role of the doctor and gives the patient simple instructions and advice. (Note: This activity can be a lot of fun if both the "patients" and the "doctors" use their imaginations to come up with silly ailments and silly advice.)

■ Have pairs perform their role plays for the class. If time allows, take a vote to determine the best (or the funniest) conversation. (10–15 minutes)

13 A visit to Mount Rushmore

Topic/functions: Direction words; asking for and giving directions

Structures: Opposites of adjectives, adverbs, and prepositions

Summary

This sequence opens with shots of the famous American monument Mount Rushmore in South Dakota. We then see a couple, Jim and Susan, packing up their belongings in a motel room. Susan seems anxious to get started on their trip to Mount Rushmore, but Jim points out that they have neither a map nor film for their camera. Although the gas station where they stop for a map doesn't sell maps, the attendant gives them directions from the station to Mount Rushmore. After buying film and stopping again to get something to eat, Susan and Jim finally set out for Mount Rushmore. As they drive down the highway, we see their frustration grow as they realize that they are hopelessly lost. Finally, after driving in circles for what must be several hours, they see the Mount Rushmore sign. By the time they drive into the parking lot, however, night has fallen. They get back into the car and decide to return to Mount Rushmore the following day, when they'll know exactly how to get there.

Cultural note

Mount Rushmore National Memorial is located in South Dakota, a state in the midwestern region of the United States. The memorial contains sculptures of four U.S. presidents: George Washington, Thomas Jefferson, Abraham Lincoln, and Theodore Roosevelt. Designed by Gutzon Borglum, the sculptures of the presidents' faces were carved out of granite into the face of Mount Rushmore and took 14 years to complete (1927–1941).

 **Preview**

1 VOCABULARY Directions

This activity introduces some of the vocabulary often used for giving directions (the functional focus of the sequence); students also practice map-reading skills.

■ Books closed. Tell students to follow the directions you give them. Have two or three students stand up. Direct the students around the room, using sentences such as, "Go to the board. Turn left and go to the window."

■ Check students' comprehension of the compass directions *north, south, east,* and *west.* To do this, establish the compass directions in your classroom. Then repeat the procedure above with directions using *north, south, east,* and *west.*

■ Books open. Explain the task. Then lead students through the four sets of directions, modeling them and having students repeat after you with correct stress and pronunciation. Finally, have students look at the example as you hold up your book and follow the route on map c.

■ Have students, working alone, complete the task. Then put them into pairs to compare answers.

■ After going over the answers with the class, review direction words as necessary.

Answers

1) c   3) d
2) b   4) a

2 WHAT DO YOU SEE?

In these activities, students prepare to watch the video by using their own general knowledge combined with visual information from the sequence to answer questions about Mount Rushmore.

(procedure continues on next page)

A Books open. Tell students to look at the photo. Then ask, "What U.S. presidents can you think of?" Have students call out their answers.

■ Explain the task, and lead students through the list of presidents' names in the box. Find out what students know about these four U.S. presidents. If it turns out that no one knows very much, point out to students that they will not need any background information in order to understand this sequence.

■ Play the first minute of the sequence with the sound either on or off (stop the video when Susan picks up the South Dakota travel brochure) as students work either alone or in pairs to write their answers. If students aren't familiar with any of the presidents in the photo, encourage them simply to guess. Tell students to use their own common sense and logic to answer the question.

■ After students compare answers in pairs or small groups, tell them to turn to page 66 in their books and to correct their answers as necessary. Then go over the answers with the class.

Answers
1) Washington
2) Jefferson
3) Roosevelt
4) Lincoln

B Books open. Explain the task, and ask students to try to answer the question before viewing. After students compare predictions in pairs, play the first minute of the sequence again.

■ After students work alone to check their prediction, have them compare answers with a partner. Finally, check answers around the class, and replay this segment of the sequence if needed.

Answer
South Dakota

Optional activity

■ *Class activity* Books closed. Write the following on the board, and explain that these are the major sections, or regions, of the United States: *Northeast, Northwest, Southeast, Southwest, Midwest, West,* and the *Rocky Mountain Region.* (Note: There is some disagreement as to the exact names of these regions, as well as about the states that are part of each region.)

■ Ask, "What part of the U.S. is South Dakota in?" (The Midwest.) Ask students if they know the names of states in any of the other areas. Write them on the board as students call out the names. Then, if time allows, tell students to come up to the front of the room to check their ideas against a map of the U.S. (5 minutes)

 Watch the video

3 GET THE PICTURE

In this activity, students watch and listen to the entire sequence to put events in the proper order.

■ Books open. Explain the task, and tell students to look at the five photos. Then say, "Now we'll watch the entire sequence with the sound on to find out what happens in the story." (Note: Students should not read the accompanying sentences at this point.)

■ Books closed. Tell students to watch with their books closed. Then play the entire sequence with the sound on.

■ Books open. Have students work alone to order the pictures. Then quickly go over the sentences, answering any questions that students may have about vocabulary or content.

■ Have students work alone to write the correct sentence under each picture. Ask students to compare answers with their neighbors, and then check answers around the class.

Answers (from left to right)
3 They stop for a snack.
1 Susan and Jim ask for directions at a gas station.
4 They drive east on Highway 44 and get lost.
2 Jim buys some film.
5 They see a sign for Mount Rushmore.

Optional activity

Pair work Books open. Put students into pairs to think of an appropriate sentence that either Susan or Jim might say in the situation shown in each photo. Circulate to offer help and to check for accuracy. Have selected pairs share their sentences with the class. (5–10 minutes)

Possible answers
1) Jim: How do we get to Mount Rushmore?
2) Jim: I have the film.
3) Jim: I feel better now. Let's go to Mount Rushmore.
4) Susan: Jim, I think we're lost.
5) Susan: Look, there's a sign for Mount Rushmore.

4 WATCH FOR DETAILS

In this activity, students watch and listen for specific information needed to answer questions about Susan and Jim's trip to Mount Rushmore.

■ Books open. Explain the task. Then read through the items with students, going over vocabulary as needed.

■ Books closed. Play the sequence with the sound on. Remind students to watch and listen for information that will help them complete the sentences.

■ Books open. Have students, working individually, complete the sentences and then compare answers with a partner.

■ Check answers around the class. If there are errors, replay the sequence so that students can check and correct their answers.

Answers
1) it's late.
2) to get a map.
3) [map b]
4) a store.
5) Wendy's.

 *Follow-up*

5 DIRECTIONS

These communicative activities give students valuable practice with asking for and giving directions.

A *Pair work* Books open. Explain the task, and ask students to look at the three pictures.

■ Go over the model dialog with students. Then put students into pairs to take turns asking for and giving directions to Mount Rushmore. As students work, circulate to offer help and to check for accuracy.

■ To help students check their answers, refer them back to map b in Exercise 4 on page 51. Then play the segment of the sequence showing the man at the gas station. Finally, ask selected pairs to share their directions with the class.

Possible answer
Take Highway 44 west, out of town. Then turn/go left on 385. Then take 244 east, and follow the signs to Mount Rushmore.

B *Pair work* Books open. As students look at the photos, ask if anyone knows where the Grand Canyon and Disneyland are (in Arizona and California). Lead students through the cues, answering any vocabulary or content questions.

■ Have students first work individually to use the given cues to plan out their directions. Then put students into pairs to take turns giving their directions. As students work, circulate to give help and encouragement.

■ After students compare answers in small groups, call on several students to share their directions with the rest of the class.

Possible answers
Take Highway 180 north./Go north on Highway 180. Then follow the signs to Grand Canyon Village.

Take Highway 5 south./Go south on Highway 5. Then turn/go right on Ball Road. Then turn/go left on West Street to Disneyland.

C *Group work* Books open. Explain the task, and lead students through the expressions in the box; also go over the model dialog.

■ Put students into groups of three to choose two places near the school. As groups work together to write their directions, circulate to offer help.

■ Tell each group to join another group to take turns telling each other their directions. Tell groups to listen to each other and then to give alternate directions to each destination.

Language close-up

6 WHAT DID THEY SAY?

This cloze activity develops bottom-up listening skills by having students complete the first conversation between Jim and Susan.

■ Books open. Tell students, working alone or in pairs, to read through the conversation and fill in any blanks they can before watching the sequence.

■ Play this segment of the sequence as many times as needed. Have students check their predictions and complete the task as they watch.

■ Have students compare answers with a partner before going over the answers as a class.

■ Model the conversation, or lead a choral repetition of it to prepare for pair work. Then put students into pairs to practice the conversation. Remind students to use the "Look Up and Say" technique. Finally, have selected pairs act out the conversation for the class.

Answers
Susan: All **right**. I think that's **everything**.
      Are you **ready** to go?
Jim: I think so. Um . . . **wait**.
Susan: What?
Jim: **Where's** the map?
Susan: What **map**?
Jim: The map to Mount Rushmore.
Susan: I don't **have** a map.
Jim: Well, **me** neither.
Susan: Well, we can **buy** one at a **gas** station.
      Let's go!
Jim: **First**, we need film.
Susan: Not **now**. We can get some later. Let's **go**.
      OK? It's already **three** o'clock. I want to
      see Mount Rushmore.
Jim: **OK**, let's go.

Optional activity
Pair work Books closed. Have students close their books and work in pairs to act out the conversation between Susan and Jim. Tell students that they do not have to use the characters' exact words, but should try to follow their actions as closely as possible. (5 minutes)

7 OPPOSITES *Giving directions*

In this activity, students continue practicing the language commonly used for giving directions.

■ Books closed. Put the following words on the board in two columns: In the first column, write *short*, *good*, *big*, *boring*; in the second column, write *small*, *tall*, *interesting*, *bad*.

■ Tell students to match opposites in the two columns. Have students call out their answers while you draw lines between the opposites as they're called out.

■ Books open. As students look at the illustration, ask, "What do you think the man is doing? What is the woman doing?" (He's asking for directions. She's giving directions.)

■ Explain the task, and lead students through the six incomplete conversations. Answer any vocabulary questions.

■ Have students work alone to fill in the missing words. Tell students to compare answers with a partner by practicing the conversations. Circulate to help and to check for accuracy. Then check answers around the class, and review as necessary.

Answers
1) south
2) right
3) down
4) west
5) behind
6) near/close

Optional activity
■ ***Pair work*** Books open or closed. Have students work in pairs to draw a map of the neighborhood around the school – but with three buildings in the wrong places. Then have each pair write three false statements about the places on the map, using words that are opposite to the correct ones.

■ Have students exchange maps and statements with another pair, and correct each other's false statements. As students work, circulate to offer help and encouragement. (10 minutes)

14 Home alone

Topic/function: Weekend activities; talking about activities in the recent past

Structure: Past tense of regular and irregular verbs

Summary

This sequence starts out in a school cafeteria during lunch. Rick joins his friend George. When George asks Rick about his weekend, Rick tells the story of what happened when his parents left him alone for the day: A pizza caught fire because Rick put it in the oven and then forgot about it when he called a friend; he had to clean up after the firefighters left a mess in the kitchen; then Rick damaged the garage when he drove his father's new car into the garage door. And George's weekend? It was "fantastic"!

 Preview

1 VOCABULARY
Weekend activities

In this exercise, students work with language used to describe common weekend activities; after matching activities described in the past tense with pictures of people involved in the activities, students exchange information about their own weekends.

A Books closed. Ask, "What do you usually do on weekends?" Have students call out their answers while you write them on the board.

■ Books open. Explain the task. Then model the sentences for the students, having them repeat after you with correct stress and pronunciation. (Note: These sentences are useful for stress practice. Have students mark the stressed sounds in each sentence. Then call on volunteers to read the sentences aloud again.)

■ Have students work alone to match the sentences with the appropriate pictures. Then, after students compare answers in pairs, check answers around the class.

Answers

1) d	4) f
2) b	5) c
3) a	6) e

Optional activity

■ *Group work* Books open. Have students rank the activities shown in the pictures according to their interest. Tell the class, "Number the pictures from one to six. Put a 1 for the activity that you like the most and a 6 for the activity that you don't like at all."

■ Put students into groups to compare their rankings. Encourage them to give reasons for their opinions.

■ Write the picture letters on the board (a–f), and tally the rankings that each one received. Do most of the students like to talk to their friends on the phone? Do most of the students hate to clean the house? (10 minutes)

B Books open. Explain the task, and lead students through the list of activities. Answer any vocabulary questions that arise.

■ Have students work alone to circle their answers. Tell them they will talk about their answers in the next part of the exercise.

C *Pair work* Books open. Explain the task, and read aloud the sample dialog. If you wish, have students repeat after you with correct stress and intonation.

■ Put students into pairs to take turns asking and answering questions about their weekends, using the activities in part B. Encourage students to ask and answer follow-up questions to get more information. Circulate to offer help and to check for accuracy. If you think students need the support, write some sample follow-up questions on the board – for example:

What movie did you see?
What did you buy?
What did you do?
What did you make?
Where did you eat?
When did you start/finish work?

2 WHAT DO YOU SEE?

In this activity, students prepare to watch the sequence by using visual information to make a prediction about the story.

▪ Books open. Have students look at the picture. Ask, "How old do you think this young man is?" (He's probably sixteen or seventeen.) Have students call out their guesses.

▪ Put students into pairs, and ask them to look at the photo and guess "what Rick did next." Ask selected students to report their predictions to the class. Accept all answers at this point.

▪ Tell students that they will watch the beginning of the video sequence and that they should check their prediction against what they see.

▪ Play the first minute of the video sequence with the sound on (until Rick says, "And then I called Julia.") as students watch and check their predictions.

▪ Check answers around the class, accepting all reasonable answers. Explain to students that any doubts will be cleared up as they continue watching the sequence.

 Watch the video

3 GET THE PICTURE

In these activities, students watch and listen to check the prediction that they made in Exercise 2 and to determine the correct order of the events in the sequence.

A Books open. Explain the task, and have students turn back to Exercise 2 on page 54.

▪ Play the first part of the sequence again, this time stopping after Rick sees that there is smoke in the kitchen. Have students check and correct their prediction while viewing.

▪ After students compare answers with a partner, check answers around the class by asking, "What did Rick do next?" and having students call out the answer.

Answer
He burned the pizza.

B Books open. Explain the task, and tell students to look at the photos. Then have

students, working individually or in pairs, predict the order of the pictures before watching the sequence. (Note: Students should not read the accompanying sentences at this point.) Have students compare predictions.

▪ Play the entire sequence with the sound on. As they watch, have students work individually to check and correct their predictions.

▪ Have students compare answers and then work together to match the sentences and the pictures. Check answers around the class.

Answers (from left to right)
2 Rick talked to his friend Julia.
6 Rick drove his father's car.
1 Rick watched TV.
5 Rick cleaned up the kitchen.
3 A fire started in the kitchen.
4 Rick called for help.

Optional activity

Pair work Books open. Put students into pairs to think of an appropriate thought that Rick might be having in each photo. Model this by saying, "In picture one, Rick is thinking, 'I'm hungry, and this show is boring. I'm going to make the pizza now.'" Circulate to help and to encourage students to be creative. Call on volunteers to share their answers with the class. (10 minutes)

Possible answers
1) I'm hungry, and this show is boring. I'm going to make the pizza now.
2) Julia is really funny. I like her a lot.
3) Oh no! The pizza! The kitchen is on fire!
4) My parents are going to be very angry.
5) What a mess!
6) Oh no! The garage door! My father's new car! He's going to be very angry.

4 WATCH FOR DETAILS

In this activity, students focus more closely on details in the story by watching and listening for information about Rick's terrible weekend.

▪ Books open. Explain the task, and read through the four items with the class. Answer any vocabulary or content questions that students may have.

- Play the video sequence, and have students check (✓) the correct answers as they watch.

- Replay the sequence if needed, and then have students compare their answers with a partner. Check answers around the class.

Answers
1) He called a friend.
2) The fire department.
3) To the store.
4) He's going to buy a new garage door.

Optional activity

- *Class activity* Books closed. Fast-forward the sequence from the beginning. From the moment you start fast-forwarding, have students count down from three (3, 2, 1). When they reach number one, stop the video and freeze the frame. Then point to a student and ask, "What happened here?" Have the student describe what happened, using the past tense.

- Repeat the process until you reach the end of the sequence. As you proceed, you might want to have the student who just answered select the next student to answer. (10 minutes)

Follow-up

5 *ROLE PLAY*

This activity gives students the chance to demonstrate and strengthen comprehension, and to be creative by acting out the story from the video.

- *Pair work* Books open. Have students look at the photo of Rick and George. Ask, "Where are Rick and George?" Elicit that they are probably in their school cafeteria.

- Explain the task, and lead students through the expressions in the box and the sentence beginnings under the seven photos. Then go over the model conversation opener, and answer any questions that students may have about the task.

- Put students into pairs to take turns playing the roles of George (speaker A) and Rick (speaker B). Tell partners to sit across from each other and to try to use facial expressions and hand gestures while doing the role play. Also, remind the students who are playing the role of George to comment on Rick's story and to ask questions.

- As students work, circulate to offer help and encouragement. When all the pairs are finished, have selected pairs perform a part of their role play for the class. Stop each pair after a few lines, and have another pair take over.

Possible answer

George: So how was your weekend?
Rick: My weekend? It was terrible!
George: What happened?
Rick: Do you really want to know?
George: Of course.
Rick: Well, my mom and dad went away for the day.
George: Yeah?
Rick: They left at one o'clock, and I was hungry. So I put a pizza in the oven.
George: Uh-huh.
Rick: And then I called Julia. We talked for about an hour.
George: Uh-oh.
Rick: Uh-oh is right. There was a fire in the kitchen.
George: Really? So what did you do?
Rick: I ran back upstairs, and I called the fire department.
George: Did a fire truck come?
Rick: Yes, it did. There was water all over the floor, so I cleaned it up.
George: So then what did you do?
Rick: Well, I was hungry, so I went to the store.
George: Uh-huh.
Rick: And I drove there in my dad's new car.
George: Oh no!
Rick: Oh, yes. I drove the car into the garage door.
George: Was your father angry?
Rick: My parents came home late, but my mother thanked me.
George: She thanked you?
Rick: Yes. She said, "The kitchen is so clean!"

6 GEORGE'S WEEKEND

In these extension activities, students get additional practice in talking about weekend activities, using the past tense (the grammatical focus of the unit).

A Pair work Books closed. Ask, "How was George's weekend?" Elicit the word *fantastic*, and write it on the board. Ask, "Did any of you have a fantastic weekend? Tell us about it." Have students call out their answers.

■ Books open. Explain the task, and put students into pairs to think up five things that George may have done. As students work, circulate to help with vocabulary and content.

■ Once students have written their five activities, have them take turns playing the roles of Rick and George to talk about George's weekend. Remind the students playing Rick to respond to what George says by making comments and asking questions.

B Class activity Books open. Read the instructions, and then have the pairs share their conversations with the class. Finally, have the class vote for the pair with the best ideas for a fantastic weekend.

Language close-up

7 WHAT DID THEY SAY?

This cloze activity develops bottom-up listening skills by having students complete the conversation from the opening scenes of the sequence.

■ Books open. Call students' attention to the photos. Ask students if they remember what Rick's father is giving Rick in the lower picture (his aunt's phone number).

■ Have students, working individually or in pairs, read through the conversation and fill in any blanks they can before watching the sequence.

■ Play this segment of the sequence as many times as necessary while students work alone to check their predictions and fill in the remaining blanks.

■ Have students compare answers with a partner.

Then have selected students read aloud lines of the conversation as you write the answers on the board.

■ Put students into groups of four to practice the conversation. Circulate to check students' stress and intonation.

Answers

George: Hi, Rick. How was your **weekend**?
Rick: My **weekend**? It was **terrible**!
George: Really? What **happened**?
Rick: Do you really want to **know**?
George: Of course!
Rick: Well, on **Saturday**, my mom and dad **went** away for the day.
George: Yeah? . . .
Mom: There's a **pizza** in the **refrigerator**.
Rick: Uh-huh.
Dad: And here's the **number** at Aunt Helen's.
Rick: **Thanks**, Dad.
Mom: **Cook** the pizza for **fifteen** minutes.
Dad: See you at **eleven** tonight.
Mom: And don't **burn** it.
Rick: **OK**. All right. See you **tonight**. Bye.

Optional activity

■ **Pair work** Books open. Divide the class in half. Tell half of the students to work in pairs to role-play the situation of Rick telling his father that he hit the garage door. Have the other half work in pairs to role-play the situation of Rick telling his mother what happened to the pizza. As students work, circulate to help and to check for accuracy.

■ After students practice their conversations, have several pairs perform their role plays for the class. (10 minutes)

Possible answers

Rick: Dad, I have bad news.
Dad: What is it, Rick?
Rick: Well, I had a little accident.
Dad: What happened?
Rick: I was hungry, so I went to the store.
Dad: Uh-huh.
Rick: I drove your new car.
Dad: That was a bad idea.
Rick: I know. And when I got home, I drove the car into the garage door.
Dad: Really?
Rick: Yes. But don't worry. I'm going to get a job, and I'm going to buy a new garage door.
Dad: Yes, you are!

Rick: Mom, I have bad news.
Mom: Yes?
Rick: Well, I burned the pizza.
Mom: That's OK.
Rick: Well, there was a fire in the kitchen. The fire department came and put out the fire.
Mom: But the kitchen is so clean.
Rick: It's clean because I cleaned up the water. I worked for two hours.
Mom: Well, it looks great. Thanks!
Rick: You're welcome.

8 PAST TENSE
Talking about the weekend

To reinforce the important structure featured in this sequence, students practice the past tense by completing conversations and then talking about their own weekends.

A Books open. Have students look at the picture. Ask, "What did this girl do last weekend?" Have students call out their answers while you write them on the board. Accept any answers that are logical and grammatically correct.

■ Explain the task, and read through the four conversations with the class. Answer any questions about vocabulary and content.

■ Have students work alone to fill in the blanks with the correct past tense forms. Then put students into pairs to compare answers.

■ Check answers around the class. Then review the structure as needed.

■ Have students practice the conversations in pairs.

Answers

1) A: **Did** you **do** anything on Saturday afternoon?
   B: Yes. I **went** to the gym and **exercised**.

2) A: **Did** you **go** out on Saturday night?
   B: Yes. I **went** to a party. We **had** a great time. And I **met** some new friends there.

3) A: **Did** you **do** something on Sunday?
   B: In the morning, I **stayed** in and **cleaned** my apartment. In the afternoon, I **saw** a movie.

4) A: **Did** you **stay** home on Sunday night?
   B: Yes, I **did**. I **wrote** some letters and **read** the newspaper.

B *Pair work* Books open. Explain the task. Then have students practice the conversations in part A again, this time substituting their own information.

Optional activity

■ *Group work* Books closed. Tell students to plan a perfect weekend, with some time spent at home and some time spent out. Put students into groups, and tell them to choose one group member to be the secretary.

■ Tell the class that each group is going to share their weekend plans with the class. After they listen to each group's plans, the rest of the class will try to agree on a rating of the weekend based on a scale of 1 to 10, with 10 being the best. Point out that groups cannot rate their own weekend.

■ Have each group share their weekend plans with the class. Then give the class a few minutes to agree on a rating. Once all the groups have shared their plans with the class, tally the ratings on the board. Which group planned the best weekend of all? (15–20 minutes)

15 Hollywood then and now

Topics/function: The history of the movie industry, getting a job in the movies; giving personal information

Structures: Past tense of *be*; Wh-questions with *did*, *was*, and *were*

Summary

This sequence takes place in Hollywood, California. Jim Hodson, a reporter, talks briefly about the history of moviemaking from the days of silent movies until the present. He then talks about the many people who come to Hollywood from all over the U.S. and from all over the world, some as tourists and others with dreams of success in the movie industry. Finally, we hear interviews with six people who have come to live in Hollywood with hopes of making it big in the movies.

 *Preview*

1 VOCABULARY *Making movies*

This activity introduces some phrases associated with moviemaking.

▪ Books closed. As a warm-up to the activity, ask, "Who likes to go to the movies?" Have students respond with a show of hands. Then ask, "Who likes old movies?" Again, have students respond with a show of hands.

▪ Books open. Read the instructions, and lead students through the phrases in the box. Then go over the example. Explain that some of the phrases could go with more than one picture, but that students should find the best match.

▪ Have students work alone or in pairs to match the phrases with the pictures and then compare answers with a partner.

▪ Check answers around the class.

Answers
1) a classic film
2) a silent film
3) black and white
4) a movie with sound
5) in color

Optional activity

Books open. Ask students if they recognize the classic film depicted in the first picture (*E.T.–The Extra-Terrestrial*). How many students have seen the movie? Did they enjoy it? (5 minutes)

2 STARS THEN AND NOW

In these activities, students first match the names of famous movie stars with their pictures; then students talk about their own preferences concerning actors and movies.

A Books open. Explain the task. Then have students work in pairs. Tell them to cover the names of the stars and to look only at the photos. How many of the movie stars can they identify?

▪ Read the names in the list, having students repeat with correct pronunciation. Then have students work alone to check their predictions and complete the task. After students compare answers in pairs, go over the answers with the class.

Answers
1, 5, 4, 3, 6, 2

Optional activity

Books open. Ask students if they know the titles of any movies that these actors and actresses starred in. (5 minutes)

B *Pair work* Books open. Explain the task, and read through the questions with students. Put students into pairs to take turns asking and answering the questions.

Optional activity

■ *Group work* Books closed. Ask students to call out different kinds of movies – for example, dramas, romances, comedies, science-fiction movies, action films – and write their ideas on the board.

■ Tell students to imagine that they are actors and actresses, and to think about the kinds of movies they would want to star in.

■ Put students into groups to tell one another about the kinds of films that they would prefer to work in if they were movie stars. As you circulate to help with vocabulary, encourage students to give reasons for their preferences. (Note: It's often best to allow students to focus on communication and fluency rather than on accuracy in this type of activity.) (5–10 minutes)

3 *MOVIE QUIZ*

In this activity, students discover how much they know about the history of movies, preparing themselves for the information that they will see and hear in the sequence.

■ *Pair work* Books closed. Ask, "Who knows about the history of the movie industry?" Have students respond with a show of hands. Then say, "Let's find out. You're going to complete some sentences about movies." Explain that they may not know the answers, but they should take a guess.

■ Books open. Explain the task, and lead students through the items. Then put students into pairs to answer. Don't give away the answers at this point. Tell students that they will have a chance to check their answers later in the lesson.

4 *WHAT DO YOU SEE?*

In these activities, students first watch and listen to the first part of the sequence in order to check their predictions and, if necessary, correct their answers in Exercise 3; they then determine whether some additional statements about the history of movies are true or false.

A Books open. Have students look at the photos. Ask selected students to say which phrases from Exercise 1 would describe these movies (*black and white, a silent film, a classic film*).

■ Explain the task, and have students look at their answers to Exercise 3.

■ Play the first two minutes of the sequence with the sound on (until the reporter says, "Today Hollywood is still the home of American movies."). Have students check and correct their answers while watching.

■ Have students compare their work with a new partner. Then go over the answers with the class.

Answers
1) Hollywood.
2) 1903.
3) 1927.
4) 1939.

B Books open. Explain the task, and lead students through the three statements. Have students predict whether each statement is true or false. Encourage them to read the statements very carefully.

■ Replay the first two minutes of the sequence, again with the sound on, and have students check (✓) *True* or *False* while watching.

■ Put students into pairs to compare answers.

■ Find out if anyone needs to watch this segment of the sequence again to finish the task. Replay as needed, and then check answers around the class.

Answers
1) False
2) False
3) True

Optional activity

Pair work Books open. Put students into pairs to correct the two false statements (1 and 2). Replay the relevant segment of the video, and tell students to listen for the correct information. (5 minutes)

Answers (correct information in bold type)
1) The first movie with a story was *The Great Train Robbery*.
2) The first movie with sound was *The Jazz Singer*.

Watch the video

5 GET THE PICTURE

In this activity, students watch and listen to the second half of the sequence to find out one specific piece of information about each person interviewed: his or her hometown.

■ Books closed. Say, "Many people from different places go to live in Hollywood. Why do you think they go there?" Ask selected students to answer. At this point, accept any reasonable answers.

■ Books open. Explain the task, and lead students through the names of the cities in the chart. Have students repeat after you with correct pronunciation. Also read the people's names.

■ Play the remainder of the video sequence with the sound on (from the point where the reporter says, "Today Hollywood is still the home of American movies."). Have students work individually to complete the chart.

■ Have students compare answers with a partner. Then ask if anyone needs to watch the sequence again. Replay as necessary, and then check answers around the class.

Answers
1) Monterey
2) Sioux City
3) Denver
4) New Orleans
5) Cincinnati
6) San Diego

Optional activity

■ Books closed. Play this segment of the sequence again, and then have students each choose one of the six people to describe.

■ On the board, write the six names (Rocky, Brian R., Brian H., Rebecca, Gina, and Roberto), and compile a class description of each person. (10–15 minutes)

6 WATCH FOR DETAILS

In these activities, students watch and listen for specific information about the people interviewed in the video.

A Books open. Explain the task, and lead students through the information under each photo. Have students, working individually or in pairs, predict the answers before watching. (Note: You may want to point out that there are some items that don't have any correct sentences.)

■ Play the entire second half of the sequence with the sound on. Have students complete the task as they watch. Then have them compare answers with a partner or around the class.

Answers
1) She came to go to school.
2) He wants to be an actor.
3) Brian Holdman came to get a job in entertainment.
4) –
5) –
6) Roberto arrived less than a year ago.

B *Pair work* Books open. Explain the task, and lead students through the example.

■ Put students into pairs to compare answers as shown in the example. As students work to correct the false statements, circulate to offer help and encouragement.

■ Find out if anyone needs to watch the sequence again in order to complete the task. Replay as needed before checking answers around the class by asking selected pairs each to write an item on the board.

Answers (corrections in bold type)
1) Rocky arrived in **1987**.
   She majored in **communications**.
2) Brian Rupert arrived **two and a half** years ago.
   He works as a **security guard**.
3) He works **in the entertainment business**.
4) Rebecca came to be **an actress**.
   She's doing very well.
5) Gina arrived **four months** ago.
   She wants to get into **film production/video production**.
6) He's studying **acting**.

C *Pair work* Explain the task, and model the sample dialog with students.

■ Put students into pairs to take turns asking and answering questions about the people in part A. As students work, circulate to help and to check for accuracy.

■ When all the pairs are finished, ask several to share a question-and-answer set with the class.

Answers

1) A: Did Rocky arrive in 1990?
   B: No, she didn't. She arrived in 1987. Did she come to go to school?
   A: Yes, she did. Did she major in music?
   B: No, she didn't. She majored in communications.

2) A: Did Brian Rupert arrive six years ago?
   B: No, he didn't. He arrived two and a half years ago. Does he want to be an actor?
   A: Yes, he does. Does he work as a waiter?
   B: No, he doesn't. He works as a security guard.

3) A: Did Brian Holdman come to get a job in entertainment?
   B: Yes, he did. Does he work at a bank?
   A: No, he doesn't. He works in entertainment.

4) A: Did Rebecca come to be a singer?
   B: No, she didn't. She came to be an actress. Is she doing very well?
   A: Yes, she is.

5) A: Did Gina arrive a month ago?
   B: No, she didn't. She arrived four months ago. Does she want to get into acting?
   A: No, she doesn't. She wants to get into film production/video production.

6) A: Did Roberto arrive less than a year ago?
   B: Yes, he did. Is he studying dancing?
   A: No, he isn't. He's studying acting.

Optional activity

Group work Books open. Put students into groups of six or seven. Have each student choose one of the people interviewed without saying who the person is. Then the other group members ask yes/no and Wh-questions to find out who the person is. The student who guesses first becomes the next one to be questioned. (10 minutes)

Follow-up

7 *INTERVIEW*

In these activities, students practice the language of asking for and giving personal information in an interview situation.

A Books open. Explain the task, and lead students through the questions and answers; have students repeat after you with correct intonation and stress. Answer any vocabulary questions that students may have.

■ Have students work alone to match the questions with the answers. Then put students into pairs to compare answers.

■ Before telling students to practice the interview, check answers around the class. As pairs take turns using the questions and answers to interview each other, circulate to offer help and to check for accuracy.

Answers

1) b
2) c
3) d
4) e
5) a

B *Pair work* Books open. Explain the task, and then put students into new pairs to take turns interviewing each other using imaginary information of their own. When all students have finished, call on selected pairs to perform their interviews for the class.

Language close-up

8 *WHAT DID THEY SAY?*

This cloze activity develops bottom-up listening skills by having students complete part of the reporter's introduction as well as his first interview.

■ Books open. Tell students to work in pairs to read through the conversation and fill in any blanks they can before watching.

■ Play this segment of the sequence as many times as necessary. Have students work alone to check their predictions and fill in the remaining blanks as they watch.

■ Have students compare answers in pairs. Then play the segment again, and have students check their work individually.

■ Model the conversation, or lead a choral repetition to prepare students for pair work. Then put students back into pairs to practice the conversation. Remind them to use the "Look Up and Say" technique.

Answers

Jim: Today Hollywood is still the home of **American** movies, and each year people come to Hollywood **from** all over the **country** and the world. **Some** of them come as tourists, but some have dreams. They want to be **stars**, and they come to Hollywood to find a **job** in the **movies**. Let's **talk** with some of them. . . . Well, what's your **name**?

Rocky: Hi. **I'm** Rocky.

Jim: Rocky. **Where** are you from?

Rocky: Northern California . . . Monterey.

Jim: When did you come to southern **California**?

Rocky: I came **down** here in '87 to go to **school**.

Jim: And what was your **major**?

Rocky: Communications.

Optional activity

■ *Pair work* Books open. Have students stay in their pairs to continue the interview. Tell them to extend the interview by using their imaginations to find out more about Rocky and her life – for example: Is she married? Does she have any children? What does she do?

■ As students work, circulate to offer help and encouragement. When things start to quiet down, call on selected pairs to perform their interviews for the rest of the class. (10 minutes)

9 *PAST TENSE*
Giving personal information

In these consolidation activities, students practice using *was*, *were*, and *did* (the grammatical focus of the unit).

A Books open. Explain the task. Then introduce the grammar point by asking a few students simple past-tense questions such as, "What time did you get up this morning?"

■ Lead students through the incomplete conversation, answering any vocabulary or content questions as they arise. Then tell students to work alone to fill in the missing verb forms: *was*, *were*, or *did*. Circulate to offer help.

■ Put students into pairs to compare answers. Then go over the answers with the class by asking selected students to call out answers and write them on the board. When students have checked their answers (and corrected them, if necessary), tell them to form new pairs to practice the interview.

Answers

A: Where **did** you grow up?
B: In Australia.
A: **Did** you study music when you **were** a child?
B: Yes, I **did**. I studied the piano for five years.
A: **Were** your parents musicians, too?
B: Yes, they **were**.
A: When **did** you come to the U.S.?
B: In 1993.
A: **Did** you get a job as a musician right away?
B: Yes, I **did**. I **was** lucky. I got a job with a rock band and made my first record the first year.

B *Class activity* Books open. Explain the task, and review the example.

■ Have students, working individually or in pairs, write five additional questions. Encourage students to write both yes/no and Wh-questions. As students work, circulate to check for accuracy.

■ Have students stand and walk around, asking and answering questions with as many classmates as possible. After a few minutes, tell students to sit back down. Then ask for volunteers to share with the class any interesting or unusual information that they discovered about their classmates.

16 The perfect date

Topic/functions: Dating activities; accepting and refusing invitations, making excuses

Structure: Verb + *to* + verb

Summary

The sequence opens with Kate and her brother, Ben, sitting in the living room talking about Kate's weekend plans. Kate tells her brother about a young man, Dan, that she is hoping will call her for a date. Ben asks about the last two young men that Kate was dating, Greg and Tony. As she starts to explain why she is no longer interested in them, the phone rings. It is Kate's friend Maggie calling to invite Kate to a party she is having that evening. Kate declines the invitation with the excuse that she isn't feeling well. Kate receives two more phone calls after Maggie's, the first from Greg and the second from Tony. Both young men invite Kate to Maggie's party, but Kate refuses both invitations and gives phony excuses. When Dan finally calls and invites Kate to a concert, she is thrilled and accepts – only to discover that Dan is calling from Maggie's house and he wants to meet Kate there. As the sequence closes, we see a clearly baffled Kate wondering how to handle this difficult situation.

 *Preview*

1 VOCABULARY Dating activities

These activities introduce the language used to talk about typical dating activities.

A Books closed. Ask, "Who is married?" Have students respond with a show of hands. Then ask the unmarried students, "Who has a special friend they like to spend time with?" Again, have students respond with a show of hands. Say, "When you're out for an evening together, this special friend is your date." Write the word *date* on the board. Then say, "The evening itself is also called a *date*. Can you think of a fun dating activity?" Have students call out their answers.

■ Books open. Explain the task, and lead students through the phrases under the pictures. Answer any questions about vocabulary that students may have.

■ *Pair work* Put students into pairs to come up with two additional dating activities. Then tell them to work together to rate the activities on a scale from 1 to 7.

■ Ask selected pairs to share their ideas with the class. Find out the favorite activity by keeping a tally of students' ratings on the board.

Optional activity

Group work Books open. Put students into groups to discuss how these dating activities compare to dating activities in their own countries. Model the group discussion by giving students an example, such as, "We usually don't go to dance clubs, but we often go to parties." (5–10 minutes)

B *Group work* Books open. Explain the task, and go through the model language with the class.

■ Put students into small groups to talk about their dating preferences. As students work, circulate to offer help and to check for accuracy.

Optional activity

Group work Books open or closed. Put students into groups of five or six. Tell them to take turns pantomiming one of the dating activities in part A while other group members guess the activity. (5–10 minutes)

2 GOOD EXCUSES

These activities introduce and practice additional language that students will hear in the video; students practice extending invitations and making excuses in a communicative context.

A Books closed. Say, "I'm going to invite you somewhere, but you don't want to go. What can you say to me?" Then ask a student, "Do you want to come over today and help me clean my house?" If the student responds with "No," ask why. Continue extending your invitation until a student responds with an excuse.

■ Books open. Explain the task. Then model the six excuses, having students repeat after you with correct stress. Point out that some of these excuses seem more acceptable than others. Say, "You invite a friend to the movies. The friend says he can't go because he's reading a new book. Is that a good excuse?" Tell students to number the excuses from 1 to 6 according to how good (or believable) they are.

■ Put students into pairs to compare their ratings. Tell students to give reasons for their choices when possible.

Optional activity

Class activity Books open. Tally students' ratings from part A on the board to see which excuses are the most and least popular. Ask selected students to explain why these particular excuses are better or worse than the others. (5 minutes)

B *Pair work* Books open. Explain the task, and model the sample dialog. Point out the use of "I'm really sorry, but I can't." (Note: You may want to explain that an apology is a way of being polite, or of making sure you don't hurt the other person's feelings.)

■ Put students into pairs to take turns inviting each other to do something from the activities in Exercise 1 and refusing with an excuse from part A of Exercise 2. As students work, circulate to offer help and to check for accuracy.

■ Ask selected pairs to come to the front of the class to act out one of their exchanges.

3 WHAT DO YOU SEE?

In this activity, students prepare to watch the sequence by using visual information to make predictions about the story.

■ Books open. As students look at the photo, say, "This is Kate. She wants to go on a date with someone special. Watch the video to see if you can guess what excuses she gives her other friends."

■ Explain the task, and make sure students turn back to Exercise 2A on page 62. Then play the entire video sequence with the sound off while students lightly check (✓) in their books the excuses that they think Kate gives her friends. Do not tell students the answers at this point, but assure them that they will find out exactly what happens when they watch the sequence with the sound on.

Optional activity

Pair work Books open. Put students into pairs to discuss how old they think Kate might be. (She's a high school student, so she's probably sixteen or seventeen.) Also ask students who they think the young man with Kate is. (He's her brother.) (5 minutes)

 Watch the video

4 GET THE PICTURE

In these activities, students watch and listen to the entire sequence to find out the characters' names as well as to discover exactly what excuses Kate gives her friends.

A Books open. Explain the task. Then read the names listed, having students repeat after you with correct pronunciation. Tell students that they need to watch and listen only for people's names. Point out that they will watch again later for other information.

■ Play the entire sequence with the sound on. Have students complete the task while they watch.

■ Give students a minute to check their answers. Then put students into pairs to compare answers before going over them with the class. Replay the sequence as needed.

Answers

1) c 4) b
2) d 5) e
3) f 6) a

B Books open. Explain the task, and read through the three items. Answer any questions about vocabulary or content.

■ Have students predict the answers to the three questions and then compare their predictions with other students.

■ Play the sequence again with the sound on. Have students check their predictions, correcting any that were wrong.

■ Replay the sequence as necessary, and then have students compare answers with a partner. Before checking answers around the class, tell students to look back at their guesses in Exercise 3. How many were correct?

Answers

1) she isn't feeling well.
2) she has to study.
3) she's reading a book.

---

5 **WATCH FOR DETAILS**

In this activity, students focus more closely on details in the sequence in order to correct mistakes in statements about the story.

■ Books open. Explain the task, and read through the six statements with the class. Again, answer any questions about vocabulary or content before students begin the task.

■ Go over the example correction in number 1, and make sure students understand that all of the statements contain false information.

■ Have students work alone to correct any statements they can before watching the sequence; then tell them to compare their predictions with a partner.

■ Books closed. Play the entire sequence with the sound on.

■ Books open. Have students work alone to check their predictions and then complete the task.

■ Ask students to compare answers around the class. Circulate and check for accuracy. Replay the sequence if necessary before giving the corrected statements.

Answers (corrections in bold type)

1) Kate wants to go to a **concert** this weekend.
2) Kate and Dan are in the same **art** class.
3) Kate thinks Greg is **boring**.
4) Maggie's party is **tonight**.
5) Kate is reading a **magazine** when Tony calls.
6) Dan wants to meet Kate at **Maggie's house**.

Optional activity

Group work Books open or closed. Ask, "What do you think Kate is going to do now?" Put students into groups to make a list of at least three things that Kate can do in this difficult situation. Have groups share their ideas with the class while you write them on the board. (10 minutes)

Follow-up

6 **ROLE PLAY**
Invitations and excuses

This activity gives students the chance to demonstrate and strengthen comprehension and to be creative by acting out a scene from the video.

■ *Group work* Books open. Lead students through the instructions, and make sure they understand that their task is to act out the situations twice. Then read aloud the model beginning to the telephone conversation between Kate and Maggie.

■ Put students into groups of four. For each group, assign each member the role of one of the four characters.

■ Play the sequence, and then have groups act out the conversations, staying as close as possible to the dialog in the video.

■ When all the groups are finished acting out the conversations from the video, clap your hands and say, "Now act them out again. This time, use your own ideas."

■ After a few minutes, have each group perform one conversation for the class.

7 PLAN YOUR WEEKEND

In these communicative activities, students first plan a weekend and then practice extending and refusing invitations.

A Books open. Explain the task, and go over the information in the chart.

- Have students work alone to complete the chart. Then put them into pairs to compare answers. Ask selected students to share their activities and excuses with the class.

B *Class activity* Books open. Explain the task, and ask two volunteers to read the sample conversation aloud.

- Have students stand up and walk around the class taking turns inviting classmates to do things, refusing invitations, and giving excuses. Encourage students to be creative; also point out the importance of being polite when refusing an invitation. As you circulate to offer help, you may want to participate in the activity, too.

Language close-up

8 WHAT DID THEY SAY?

This cloze activity develops bottom-up listening skills by having students complete the opening conversation between Kate and her brother.

- Books open. Tell students to work alone to read through the conversation and fill in any blanks they can before watching. Then tell them to compare their predictions with a partner.

- Play this segment of the sequence as many times as necessary while students work alone to check their predictions and fill in the remaining blanks as they watch.

- Have students compare answers in pairs. Then play the segment again, and have students check their work.

- Model the conversation, and then lead a choral repetition of it to prepare students for pair work. Then put students into pairs to practice the conversation. You may want to remind students that Kate's voice is on the answering-machine message.

Answers

Ben: So, Kate, it's the **weekend**. **What** are you going to **do**?
Kate: I don't **know**. I really **want** to go to the Spiders **concert**, but I need a **ticket**. And Maggie's having a **party**. But –
Ben: But?
Kate: But I don't want to go. I **can't**. Dan's going to **call**.
Ben: Dan?
Kate: Yeah. He's this **great** guy in my art **class**.
Ben: But what happened to Greg? And Tony?
Kate: Oh, Greg? He's **boring**. And Tony? I don't **know**. He's kind of . . .
Ben: **Maybe** that's Dan.
Kate: Don't **answer** it. **Wait**!
Answering machine: We can't **come** to the phone right **now**. So please leave your **name** and phone **number** after the beep. We'll call you back **soon**.

Optional activity

Pair work Books open. Have students practice the conversation again. Tell them that this time Kate is asking Ben about his weekend. (10 minutes)

9 WANT TO, NEED TO, HAVE TO
Making excuses

In this consolidation activity, students practice using *want to*, *need to*, and *have to* in excuses in response to invitations.

- Books closed. Write the phrases *I want to*, *I need to*, and *I have to* on the board. Ask students to suggest endings to these sentences while you write their ideas on the board.

- Books open. Call attention to the illustration. Say, "This young man can't go out tonight. Why not?" (Because he has to study.) Have students call out their answer while you write it on the board.

- Explain the task, and read aloud the invitations and incomplete responses. Answer any vocabulary or content questions.

■ Have students work alone to write their replies to the invitations. As students are filling in the conversations, circulate to offer help and encouragement.

■ Put students into pairs to practice the conversations. Tell them to take turns inviting and responding to the invitations. If time allows, ask selected pairs to share an invitation-and-excuse set with the rest of the class.

House party

Bob and Jennifer go to their teacher's party, but things don't turn out as expected.

Jennifer: Is that it?

Bob: Um, yeah. 410 Pine Street.

Jennifer: OK.

•   •   •

Jennifer: Well, what's the apartment number?

Bob: Um . . .

Jennifer: Oh, great, Bob!

Bob: I . . . I think it's 302.

Jennifer: Really?

Bob: Yeah, 302. (*pushes intercom button*)

Voice: Hello.

Bob: Hi, it's Bob and Jennifer.

•   •   •

Bob: Oh, there it is . . . 302.

Eduardo: Hi. Come on in. I'm Eduardo.

Jennifer: Hi, Edward. Nice to –

Eduardo: It's Eduardo. E-D-U-A-R-D-O.

Jennifer: Oh, . . . Eduardo. Sorry. It's nice to meet you. I'm Jennifer.

Bob: And I'm Bob.

Eduardo: Well, it's nice to meet you. Are you, um, Terri's friends?

Jennifer: Terri?

Guest: Eduardo!

Eduardo: Oh, excuse me.

Bob: Who's Terri?

Jennifer: I don't know. I think she's Dr. Roberts's wife.

Bob: And where *is* Dr. Roberts?

Jennifer: Um . . . I don't know.

Ken: Hi. I'm Ken. Are you John's friend?

Jennifer: Uh, no, Ken, I'm his student. My name's Jennifer.

Ken: Student?

Eduardo: Ken!

Ken: Well, uh, excuse me, Jennifer.

Naomi: Excuse me, are you Eduardo?

Bob: No, I'm not. I think he's over there. My name's Bob . . . Bob Freeman.

Naomi: Nice to meet you. I'm Naomi Hernandez.

Bob: Nice to meet you. Are you in my math class?

Naomi: Math class? No, I'm a friend of Terri's.

Bob: Oh. Is Dr. Roberts here?

Naomi: Dr. Roberts? No, I don't think so.

John: Time to eat, everyone!

Terri: Yes, help yourselves.

Jennifer: That's not Dr. Roberts.

Bob: No, it's not.

Bob/Jennifer: Uh-oh!

Terri: Hi. Are you, um, Naomi's friends?

Bob: Uh, no. I'm Bob, and this is Jennifer.

Jennifer: Hi. Nice to meet you.

Terri: It's nice to meet you, too. My name is Terri and, uh, this is my husband, John.

John: Hi.

Bob: Hi. Nice to meet you.

John: Nice to meet you.

Jennifer: Hi. Is this, um, your apartment?

John: Well, yes, it is. And you are . . .

Bob: Bob Freeman.

Jennifer: And I'm Jennifer.

Bob: We're in Dr. Roberts's class.

Terri: Oh, John Roberts! He lives in Apartment 203, I think.

John: And this is Apartment 302.

Bob/Jennifer: 3-0-2!

Terri: That's OK. Please.

Bob: Oh, no . . .

John: It's no problem. Please!

Jennifer: Well, OK. Thank you.

Bob: Yes. Thanks.

Lost and found

Sandra oversleeps and has to rush to make her flight to Italy.

Anne: Sandra! Sandra, get up!

Sandra: Why?

Anne: Why? It's nine o'clock. Your flight's at eleven.

Sandra: Italy! My trip! Anne, call a taxi. . . . Oh no! Where are . . . where are my glasses?

Anne: Are they on your desk?

Sandra: Maybe. (*to herself*) The desk. Behind the tissues? No. Under the newspaper? No. In my purse? No, . . . no, . . . no, . . . Anne!

Anne: Taxi, please. . . . Yes. . . . 807 Key Street. Please hurry.

Sandra: Anne!

Anne: What?

Sandra: My glasses! They're not here.

Anne: Are they in the bathroom?

Sandra: I don't know.

Anne: No, here they are, inside your makeup bag.

Sandra: Good, thanks. (*to herself*) Now, where is my dress? (*to Anne*) Anne, where's my new dress?

Anne: Your new dress?

Sandra: Yes, yes. My new dress!

Anne: It's in your suitcase. Sandra, please hurry! You're late!

Sandra: (*to herself*) Now, where's my wallet? Oh, there it is, on the television. And my passport! (*to Anne*) Anne, where's my passport?

Anne: It's there, in your purse.

Sandra: Oh, right. Thanks. And my shoes? Where are my black shoes? And my sunglasses?

Anne: Your shoes are in front of the sofa, and your sunglasses are . . . on the sofa.

Sandra: How do I look?

Anne: Great! You look great. . . . It's your taxi! . . . Have a great trip.

Sandra: OK. Thanks.

•   •   •

Sandra: Is my suitcase in the back?

Taxi driver: Suitcase?

3 Newcomer High School

At a very interesting school, students from around the world talk about their countries of origin.

Saida: Hi. My name is Saida Arrika Ekalona, and I'm here at the Newcomer High School in New York City. Students from many different countries go to this school. They speak different languages, but classes? Classes are in English.

•　　•　　•

Saida: Let's talk to some of the students and find out where they're from. . . . Hi. What's your name?

Sargis: My name is Sargis.

Saida: And what's your last name?

Sargis: My last name is Sedrakyan.

Saida: And so, where are you from?

Sargis: I come from Armenia.

Saida: Can you show me where that is on the map?

Sargis: Of course. This is Armenia, and this is the capital of Armenia, Yerevan. I am from there.

Saida: All right. And so, what language do you speak at home?

Sargis: At home, I speak Armenian.

Saida: Armenian. OK, so how do you say "Thank you" in Armenian?

Sargis: *Shnorhagalutiun.*

Saida: Thank you very much.

Sargis: You're welcome.

•　　•　　•

Saida: Hi. What's your name, and where are you from?

Abraham: I'm Abraham. I'm from Ghana.

Saida: What's your last name, Abraham?

Abraham: Kwarteng.

Saida: Can you show us where Ghana is?

Abraham: Sure. This is Ghana, and Cape Coast.

Saida: What language do you speak?

Abraham: Twi.

Saida: And how do you say "Thank you" in Twi?

Abraham: *Meda ase.*

Saida: *Meda ase. Meda ase*, Abraham.

Abraham: You're welcome.

•　　•　　•

Saida: Hi. What's your name?

Maria: Hi. My name is Maria.

Saida: Maria. And what's your last name, Maria?

Maria: Loza.

Saida: Loza.

Maria: Yes.

Saida: And where are you from?

Maria: I'm from Bolivia.

Saida: And what city in Bolivia?

Maria: La Paz.

Saida: Can you show me where that is?

Maria: Yes, here. Here is Bolivia, and this is La Paz, and it's the capital, too.

Saida: All right. And so, in Bolivia you speak Spanish at home, right?

Maria: Yeah.

Saida: All right. And so you say *"Muchas gracias,"* which means "Thank you very much."

Maria: Yes.

Saida: *Muchas gracias.*

•　　•　　•

Saida: Hi. What's your name?

Edna: My name is Edna.

Saida: Edna?

Edna: Yes.

Saida: And what's your last name?

Edna: Da Silva.

Saida: Da Silva.

Edna: Yes.

Saida: OK, so where are you from?

Edna: Brazil.

Saida: Oh, Brazil, in South America.

Edna: Yes.

(continued)

Saida: And what city in Brazil?

Edna: Vitória.

Saida: Can you show me where it is?

Edna: Yes. . . . This is Brazil. . . . Here is Vitória.

Saida: In Brazil, you speak Portuguese.

Edna: Yes.

Saida: How do you say "Thank you" in Portuguese?

Edna: *Obrigado.*

•　　•　　•

Saida: Hi. What's your name?

Gregory: Gregory.

Saida: Gregory. What's your last name, Gregory?

Gregory: Iskra.

Saida: Iskra. And so, where are you from?

Gregory: Poland.

Saida: Can you show me where it is?

Gregory: Yes. This is Poland.

Saida: Which part of Poland?

Gregory: This . . . here.

Saida: OK. And so, how do you say "Thank you" in Polish?

Gregory: *Dziekuje.*

Saida: *Dziekuje?*

Gregory: Yes.

Saida: *Dziekuje.*

•　　•　　•

Saida: Hi. What's your name?

Chen Shen: Chen Shen.

Saida: Chen Shen.

Chen Shen: Yes.

Saida: And what's your last name?

Chen Shen: Ma.

Saida: Ma. So, where are you from?

Chen Shen: China.

Saida: China. And what city in China?

Chen Shen: Guangzhou.

Saida: Can you show me where that is?

Chen Shen: OK. This is China. This is Guangzhou.

Saida: So, what language do you speak at home?

Chen Shen: Uh, Cantonese.

Saida: Cantonese.

Chen Shen: Yeah.

Saida: And how do you say "Hello" in Cantonese?

Chen Shen: *Nei ho.*

Saida: *Nei ho?* Thank you. Thank you very much.

Chen Shen: You're welcome.

•　　•　　•

Saida: Hi. What's your name?

Sadia: Sadia.

Saida: Sadia. And what's your last name, Sadia?

Sadia: Ashfaq.

Saida: And so, where are you from?

Sadia: Pakistan.

Saida: What town in Pakistan?

Sadia: In Karachi.

Saida: Can you show me where Karachi is on the map?

Sadia: Yeah, of course. This is, uh, Pakistan, and this is Karachi.

Saida: All right. And so, what language do you speak?

Sadia: Urdu.

Saida: So how do you say, uh, "Hello" in Urdu?

Sadia: *Shukria.*

Saida: *Shukria.* Thank you very much.

Sadia: You're welcome.

•　　•　　•

Saida: Oh, there's the bell. It's the end of class. Thanks, everybody.

Class: You're welcome.

Saida: This is Saida Arrika Ekalona, reporting from the Newcomer High School in New York City.

4

What are you wearing?

People in southern California talk about the clothes they have on.

Paula: Hi there. I'm Paula Keating, and it's a beautiful, sunny Wednesday morning in southern California. People are wearing suits, dresses, jeans, miniskirts, T-shirts . . . all kinds of things. Let's talk to some people about their clothes.

•   •   •

Paula: Good morning!

Man 1: Good morning.

Paula: Are you going to work?

Man 1: I *am* going to work.

Paula: And what are you wearing today?

Man 1: Today I'm wearing a black coat, white shirt, black tie, and black suspenders.

Paula: What color is your briefcase?

Man 1: I'm carrying a black briefcase with tan handles.

•   •   •

Paula: Hi there!

Woman 1: Hi.

Paula: What are you wearing today?

Woman 1: I'm wearing a T-shirt, a sweatshirt, orange leggings, white socks, and white tennis shoes.

Paula: OK . . .

Woman 1: And a white hat.

Paula: And a white hat. Oh, that's nice. Are you going to work?

Woman 1: I'm going to work *out*.

Paula: Is orange your favorite color?

Woman 1: Actually, I like orange a lot, but my favorite color is red.

•   •   •

Paula: Hello.

Woman 2: Hello.

Paula: What are you wearing today?

Woman 2: Today I'm wearing a white shirt, a beige sweater, blue jeans, dark brown boots, a dark brown belt, and also a matching brown handbag.

•   •   •

Man 2: I'm wearing a white shirt, a red and green tie, green pants, a black belt, and black shoes.

•   •   •

Woman 3: Well, I'm wearing blue slacks and, uh, another blue top.

•   •   •

Teenager: I have a pink polo shirt on.

•   •   •

Woman 4: I'm wearing a black business suit with gold buttons.

•   •   •

Paula: Hi there! What are you wearing today?

Woman 5: Uh, blue jeans and a red T-shirt.

Paula: Now, is this your favorite thing to wear?

Woman 5: Yes.

Paula: So, what do you wear to work?

Woman 5: A suit. Just like what you're wearing: a two-piece suit.

•   •   •

Paula: Hi there! What are you wearing today?

Woman 6: I'm wearing a miniskirt and tights and a turtleneck shirt.

Paula: And is this a vest?

Woman 6: Yes, it is.

Paula: And what's your favorite color?

Woman 6: Probably rose colors.

Paula: Rose, like a pink?

Woman 6: Like a pink, yes.

Paula: Now, what's your favorite thing to wear?

Woman 6: Casual clothes.

Paula: Casual, . . . like today! . . . And what am I wearing? A tan pantsuit and a yellow blouse. Why? Because it's a beautiful day. I'm Paula Keating, reporting from southern California.

5 What are you doing?

Vicki in Los Angeles and her friend Paulo in Rio de Janeiro call each other to say hello.

Vicki: Here's the guest list for our party Saturday night.

Mariko: Wow! Everyone's coming.

Vicki: Except Paulo.

Mariko: Oh, that's right. Paulo's visiting his parents in Rio. Too bad. He's really nice.

Vicki: Wait! Here's a postcard from Paulo. . . . It says he's coming back Friday.

Mariko: That's great! Let's call and invite him.

Vicki: Good idea. . . . Here's his number in Brazil.

Mariko: Wait a minute. What time is it?

Vicki: Midnight.

Mariko: What time is it in Rio?

Vicki: In Rio? I don't know.

Mariko: Hmm. . . . It's midnight in L.A., so it's . . .

Vicki: [*dials phone*] Hello? Hello?

Paulo: Hello?

Vicki: Hello, is Paulo there?

Paulo: Vicki?

Vicki: Paulo? Are you OK?

Paulo: Yes, yes, I'm fine.

Vicki: You're sleeping.

Paulo: Oh, no, I'm just getting up. It's, uh, six A.M. here.

Vicki: Six A.M.! Paulo, I'm so sorry. I –

Paulo: No, no, that's OK, Vicki. How are you?

Vicki: I'm fine. Listen, Paulo, I can call you later.

Paulo: No, Vicki. Let me call *you*.

Vicki: OK. Sorry. Bye, Paulo.

Paulo: OK, bye, Vicki. Talk to you later.

Mariko: So, how's Paulo?

Vicki: He's just getting up. It's six o'clock in the morning there. He's calling me back later.

Mariko: Where are you going?

Vicki: I'm going to bed. Good night.

Mariko: Well, good night, Vicki.

•   •   •

Vicki: [*phone rings*] Hello?

Paulo: Vicki, hi. It's Paulo!

Vicki: Paulo!

Paulo: Yes. It's nine o'clock in the morning here, and I'm having breakfast. What are *you* doing?

Vicki: What am *I* doing? Well, I'm . . .

6 Day and night

Andi introduces us to her busy life: She's a police officer during the week and a singer on the weekends.

Andi: Hi. My name's Andi. I'm twenty-three. This is my house. I live here with my mom and my dad and my sister, Susan. Susan is seventeen. She's a high school student. It's OK here, really. This is my room. Nice, huh? Weekdays, I get up about six. Then I have breakfast with my family. Then I go to work.

•   •   •

I drive to work. I'm a police officer.

•   •   •

This is the police station. I start at nine o'clock. It's a great job.

•   •   •

I work outside. I work with people.

•   •   •

At noon, I usually go to lunch.

•   •   •

At one o'clock, I work again. At five, I go home.

•   •   •

Weekday nights, I stay home. I eat dinner. I read. I watch TV. I talk with Susan. Every night is the same. But weekends are different.

•   •   •

Friday, Saturday, and Sunday, I work at Ivories. I start at nine o'clock. I'm a singer!

•   •   •

But on Monday, I'm a police officer.

93

7 Our first house

A young couple in their new home receives some surprise visitors.

Margo: I'll get it.

Chuck: Good.

Margo: Mom! Dad! What a surprise!

Margo's mother: Hi, honey. How are you? How's Chuck? These are for you.

Margo: Thank you. They're beautiful! And we're fine. Please come in.

Margo's father: We were out in the car –

Margo's mother: And we thought, "Let's go visit Margo and Chuck and see their new house."

Margo's father: And your house is . . . well, lovely.

Chuck: Mom! Dad! Hi. How are you?

Margo's mother: Hi, Chuck. Fine, thanks.

Margo's father: Hi, Chuck. Congratulations on the new house. It's perfect.

Chuck: Thanks.

Margo: Well, let me show you around. . . . Well, this is our living room.

Margo's mother: It's, um, nice, dear.

Margo's father: And these cushions are . . . comfortable.

Margo: Well, we don't have much furniture yet, but . . .

Margo's mother: Oh, that's OK.

•   •   •

Chuck: And this is the bedroom. . . .

Margo's father: Well, it's, uh, sunny.

Margo's mother: Yes, it *is* sunny.

Margo: It's great for our work.

Chuck: Yeah.

Margo: And look at this big closet.

Margo's mother: Yes, it *is* big.

Chuck: And the bathroom is here. . . .

Margo's father: Uh-huh.

Margo: Well, let's go into the kitchen.

•   •   •

Margo: And this is our kitchen.

Margo's mother: Very nice.

Margo's father: Uh-huh!

Chuck: Well, let's go into the dining room.

•   •   •

Margo's mother: What's this?

Margo: Oh, this is our table.

Chuck: I'll get some chairs.

Margo's father: Here, let me help you.

Chuck: Oh, thanks, Dad. . . . Here you go.

Margo's father: OK.

Margo: Thank you.

Margo's father: There you go.

Margo's mother: (*handing Chuck a gift*) Here, Chuck. Open this one.

Chuck: Gee, thanks, Mom.

Margo's mother: (*to Margo*) And *you* open this one.

Margo: Thanks, Mom.

Chuck: Oh, great! A tablecloth. This is perfect.

Margo: Oh, . . . look at this vase. Now we have something beautiful for our flowers. Thank you.

Chuck: Hey, Dad, want to give me a hand here?

Margo's father: Sure.

Chuck: Here we go. . . . And turn it this way. . . oh, that's perfect.

Margo's father: Isn't that nice?

Chuck: Yup. Fits just right.

Margo's father: Hey! Here's another gift for you, Chuck.

Chuck: Oh, this is too much. Thanks. . . . Oh, great!

Margo: Wow! Candles. Oh, those are nice. Thank you.

Chuck: Yes, thanks!

Margo's father: Light them up?

Chuck: Yeah.

Margo's father: There we are.

Margo: I'll make some coffee.

Margo's mother: Oh, wait! There's one more gift.

Margo's father: Well, we're not sure it's
    something you need, but –

Margo's mother: But we hope you'll like it.

Margo: Oh, it's –

Margo's mother: A picture of us!

People who work at night talk about their jobs and their rather unusual routines.

Reporter: Most people work during the day. They go to work in the morning and come home in the evening. But some people work at night. Tonight, we're going to meet some of them and find out what they do.

• • •

Reporter: People get sick or hurt at any time of the day. The hospital is always a busy place. . . . Excuse me. Can I ask you a few questions?

Dr. West: Yes.

Reporter: Are you a nurse or a doctor?

Dr. West: I'm a doctor. My name is Dr. Miguel West.

Reporter: Dr. West, when do you start work?

Dr. West: I start work at, uh, six P.M. in the evening, and we work through till eight A.M. in the morning.

Reporter: Do you like working at night?

Dr. West: I like it, but it can be tiring sometimes.

Reporter: Is it busy at night?

Dr. West: It's pretty busy.

Reporter: What do you do, exactly?

Dr. West: I'm the doctor in the emergency department.

• • •

Reporter: We're here at the *Star Tribune* newspaper. It's midnight, but everyone is working hard. . . . Excuse me.

Joe: Uh, yes?

Reporter: Can I ask you a few questions?

Joe: Yes, you can.

Reporter: What's your name?

Joe: Uh, my name is, uh, Joe Arrington.

Reporter: Can you tell me about your job?

Joe: I'm a security guard here at the *Star Tribune*.

Reporter: What time do you start work?

Joe: Oh, normally, uh, I start work about three P.M.

Reporter: And when do you finish?

Joe: About, uh, eleven P.M.

• • •

Reporter: What's your name?

Hylaria: My name is Hylaria Perez.

Reporter: What is your job here at the newspaper?

Hylaria: I'm an editor.

Reporter: An editor? What does an editor do?

Hylaria: Well, I write articles for our newspaper, and I also correct other people's, um, articles.

Reporter: What time do you start work?

Hylaria: I start work at about four P.M.

Reporter: What time do you go home?

Hylaria: I go home, you know, when the paper's done, and that usually happens about one-thirty in the morning.

Reporter: Do you like working nights?

Hylaria: Yes, I love working at nights. I don't have to wake up early in the morning.

• • •

Reporter: This police station is open twenty-four hours a day. Many police officers work the night shift. . . . Excuse me.

Officer Kuyper: Hi.

Reporter: What's your name?

Officer Kuyper: I'm Officer Scott Kuyper.

Reporter: Can you tell me what you do?

Officer Kuyper: I'm a police officer.

Reporter: Is your job dangerous?

Officer Kuyper: Uh, sometimes, but most of the time it's pretty safe.

Reporter: Do you always work in your car?

Officer Kuyper: Yes, most of the time.

Reporter: And what time do you start work?

Officer Kuyper: I start at three o'clock in the afternoon.

Reporter: And what time do you finish?

Officer Kuyper: I usually finish at eleven P.M. at night.

Reporter: Do you like working at night?

Officer Kuyper: I love working at night.

Reporter: Why?

Officer Kuyper: Oh, I'm not really a morning person, and I like the activity level on the three-to-eleven shift. I love this time of day.

Reporter: Well, thank you!

Officer Kuyper: You're welcome.

• • •

Reporter: It's about six A.M. This donut shop is full of people. Let's go in and talk with some of them. . . . Excuse me.

Eric: Hi there.

Reporter: What's your name?

Eric: Eric.

Reporter: Eric, do you work during the day?

Eric: No, I work at night.

Reporter: And what do you do?

Eric: I make donuts.

Reporter: What kind of donuts do you make?

Eric: White donuts, sprinkled donuts, chocolate donuts, vanilla donuts . . .

Reporter: What's your favorite kind of donut?

Eric: Uh, chocolate.

Reporter: What time do you start work?

Eric: Midnight.

Reporter: Midnight? And when do you finish?

Eric: About seven in the morning.

• • •

Steve: Can I have a chocolate donut and a cup of coffee, please? . . .

Reporter: Good morning.

Steve: Good morning.

Reporter: Can I ask you a few questions?

Steve: Yeah, sure.

Reporter: Are you going to work?

Steve: No, I just finished.

Reporter: Oh. What do you do?

Steve: I'm a janitor. I clean offices downtown.

Reporter: When do you work?

Steve: Well, I start at about ten P.M., and I finish at six in the morning. I work about eight hours.

Reporter: So, what do you do during the day?

Steve: I'm a student. I have classes at the university.

Reporter: Do you like working at night?

Steve: Uh, yeah, it's OK.

Reporter: Why?

Steve: I can do my homework during the day.

Reporter: Well, good luck in school! . . . And my job? Sometimes it's a night job, too. This is Lori Aoki reporting. Good night *and* good morning.

9 What are you having for breakfast?

People in a restaurant talk about what they are eating and drinking for breakfast.

Neil: Hi. I'm Neil Murray, and this is my breakfast. I'm having scrambled eggs, bacon, toast, coffee, and orange juice. This is a very traditional breakfast in the United States, but people here eat lots of other things for breakfast, too. . . . Let's talk to some people about their breakfasts.

• • •

Neil: Good morning. What are you having for breakfast?

Woman 1: I'm having a bagel with cream cheese and hot tea with lemon.

Neil: Do you always have tea for breakfast?

Woman 1: Yes, I have hot tea with lemon all day long.

• • •

Neil: Good morning.

Woman 2: Well, good morning.

Neil: What are you having for breakfast?

Woman 2: I'm starting out with a bowl of fruit. I like to begin my day with a good breakfast.

Neil: What fruit do you have in your bowl?

Woman 2: This morning, I have grapes, watermelon, bananas, and honeydew melon.

Neil: Do you always have fruit for breakfast?

Woman 2: Yes.

Neil: What else are you having?

Woman 2: This morning, I will have bacon and eggs and toast.

• • •

Neil: And what are you having?

Man 1: I'm having fresh fruit.

Neil: A small breakfast.

Man 1: Um, . . . an average breakfast for me.

Neil: Do you ever have eggs for breakfast?

Man 1: Not very often anymore.

Neil: What are you drinking?

Man 1: I'm drinking coffee.

• • •

Man 2: I'm having some French toast, bacon, and coffee.

Neil: Do you always have French toast for breakfast?

Man 2: Sometimes I do. Sometimes I have an egg omelette with, uh, ham or bacon or sausage, along with my coffee.

• • •

Neil: Good morning.

Man 3: Good morning.

Neil: What are you having for breakfast?

Man 3: Actually, I'm having pancakes with, uh, bananas, nuts, some blueberries in them, a little coffee and cream, plenty of butter.

• • •

Neil: And what are you having?

Woman 3: I'm having fried eggs and toast, and coffee, and orange.

Neil: Is this what you normally have for breakfast?

Woman 3: No, normally I just have coffee.

Neil: Do you ever have bacon for breakfast?

Woman 3: No, very rarely.

• • •

Neil: Good morning. What are you having for breakfast?

Woman 4: I'm having cold cereal with apple juice and hot chocolate.

Neil: Do you always have cold cereal for breakfast?

Woman 4: No, sometimes I have scrambled eggs.

• • •

Neil: Excuse me. What are you having for breakfast?

Woman 5: I'm having yogurt and English muffin, with hot tea.

Neil: What's in it?

Woman 5: It looks like it has blueberries and walnuts and bananas.

Neil: And what are you having right here?

• • •

98

Woman 5: This is an English muffin with, I guess, butter. Maybe I'll put on peanut butter.

•   •   •

Neil: Mmm, this looks good. What is it?

Woman 6: This is a Mexican omelette.

Neil: What's in it?

Woman 6: Well, besides your eggs, uh, we have jalapeño peppers, sour cream, green onions, salsa. It's very delicious.

•   •   •

Waitress: More coffee?

Neil: Thank you.

Waitress: You're welcome.

Neil: This is Neil Murray reporting from The Egg and I Restaurant. Have a good day.

People talk about the activities that they enjoy at the Chelsea Piers Sports and Entertainment Center in New York City.

Mary: Hi! This is Mary Purdy, and today I'm in New York City at the Chelsea Piers Sports and Entertainment Center. There are a lot of different kinds of things to do here. You can play soccer or basketball. You can go ice-skating or Rollerblading. You can practice your swing. You can do gymnastics. You can swim or lift weights. You can even go rock climbing. Let's go talk to some of the people who are here today. Come on!

•   •   •

Woman 1: Hi.

Mary: Hi. So what are you doing here today?

Woman 1: I'm here with my sister-in-law.

Mary: And right now you're Rollerblading?

Woman 1: Yes, I am.

Mary: Can you ice-skate?

Woman 1: No.

Mary: But you can Rollerblade.

Woman 1: Yes, I can.

Mary: Can you Rollerblade backwards for us?

Woman 1: Yes, I can.

Mary: Let's see.

Woman 1: OK.

Mary: Very good!

•   •   •

Mary: So, what are you doing here today?

Man 1: I'm doing some Rollerblading and hitting some golf balls . . .

Mary: Is this your first time Rollerblading?

Man 1: Yeah.

Mary: Uh-huh. So what's your favorite sport?

Man 1: I like to golf a lot. Golf is good.

•   •   •

Mary: Hey, you guys, this looks . . . looks like a lot of fun. What are you doing here?

Man 2: Oh, rock climbing.

Mary: Rock climbing?

Man 2: Yeah.

Mary: Wow, that sounds exciting!

Man 2: Yeah, it is.

Mary: Is this a fun sport?

Man 2: It's a fantastic sport.

Mary: Is it? And is it dangerous?

Man 2: At times, yes.

Mary: Well, let's see what you can do. You want to rock climb for us?

Man 3: Yeah, sure.

Mary: All right. Great. Thanks.

•   •   •

Mary: What are you guys doing here today?

Child 1: Um, skating.

Mary: Skating? Is skating your favorite sport?

Child 2: Yes.

Mary: How often do you come here?

Child 1: Um, every Friday.

Mary: Every Friday. And wh-what else do you do here in Chelsea Piers?

Child 2: Um, you could go roller-skating outside.

Mary: So, what other sports do you play?

Child 1: They have rock climbing, and I could do that, too.

•   •   •

Mary: How often do you come here?

Man 4: About two, three times a week.

Mary: Are you a good skater?

Man 4: No, no.

•   •   •

Mary: So, what are you doing here today?

Man 5: Just hitting golf balls.

Mary: Do you, uh, do you play golf often?

Man 5: Yeah, in the summer.

Mary: Yeah?

Man 5: Every week.

Mary: How do you like this place?

Man 5: Oh, it's fantastic. You don't have to bend down to put the balls on the tee.

Mary: Uh-huh.

Man 5: It comes up automatically.

•   •   •

Mary: Whoops! Looks like I need to come here a lot more often. This is Mary Purdy reporting from Chelsea Piers Sports and Entertainment Center.

A weekend in New York City

People talk about what they plan to do during their short visit to "the Big Apple."

Reporter: New York City! People come here from all over the country – and all over the world. Let's talk to some of them.

• • •

Reporter: Excuse me.

Man 1: Yes?

Reporter: Where are you two from?

Man 1: Puerto Rico.

Reporter: Puerto Rico! And what are you going to do while you're here in New York?

Man 1: Visit. . . uh. . . visit different places.

Reporter: Uh, where are you going to go?

Woman 1: Go see *Beauty and the Beast*.

Reporter: *Beauty and the Beast* . . . the musical.

Woman 1: Yes.

Reporter: Well, are you going to do anything tonight?

Man 1: Dinner.

Reporter: Are you enjoying your trip?

Man 1: Very much so, yeah.

• • •

Reporter: What's your name?

Girl 1: Megan.

Reporter: Megan. Well, where are you going?

Girl 1: To take a carriage ride.

Reporter: *(to sister)* And where are you going?

Girl 2: Well, she's my sister, so I'm going with her.

Reporter: You're going with her. And where are you from?

Girl 2: New Jersey.

Reporter: And what are you doing in New York today?

Girl 2: We're just seeing the sights.

• • •

Reporter: Hi. Where are you from?

Woman 2: We're from Ireland. We're living here in New York.

Reporter: Are you? And do you like living here?

Woman 2: We love here. It's a great city. Manhattan is wonderful. We come here every weekend.

Reporter: Uh, and where are you going right now?

Woman 2: We're going to Central Park.

Reporter: What are you going to do when you get there?

Man 2: Well, we're going to take the kids down to the park. And then they're going . . . they love the roller-skating. After that, then we take them to the zoo.

• • •

Reporter: Hi! Where are you guys from?

Teenager 1: Uh, we're from Dallas.

Reporter: Dallas, Texas. And what are you going to do today?

Teenager 2: Um, well, we're going to Central Park and the Statue of Liberty. We're here for our sixteenth birthday.

Reporter: So it's your birthday. Happy birthday! Are you going to go anywhere tomorrow, or . . .

Teenager 1: Um, they're leaving tonight, and . . .

Teenager 3: We're going to go see *Rent*.

Reporter: *Rent*, . . .

Teenager 3: Yeah.

Reporter: The Broadway show *Rent*.

Teenager 3: Yeah.

Reporter: Well, thank you very much, and have a happy birthday.

Teenagers: Thanks.

Reporter: Bye-bye.

• • •

Reporter: Excuse me.

Woman 3: Hi!

Reporter: Where are you from?

Woman 3: I'm from New York.

Reporter: You're from New York. And, uh, where are you going?

Woman 3: I'm going to the park.

Reporter: And what are you going to do?

Woman 3: I'm going to take a walk.

Reporter: Are you going anywhere tomorrow?

Woman 3: Tomorrow I'm going to run in a race.

Reporter: Wh-what kind of race?

Woman 3: It's a twenty-mile race. I'm training for the marathon.

• • •

Reporter: Hi. Where are you from?

Woman 4: Athens, Georgia.

Reporter: And where are you going today?

Woman 4: Well, right now we're getting ready to go on a bus tour . . . Big Apple bus tour.

Reporter: And where will that take you?

Woman 4: Um, primarily we're interested in the Statue of Liberty and the Empire State Building. We're here with a group of little boys.

Reporter: Hi. Where are you guys from?

Boys: Athens, Georgia.

Reporter: Athens, Georgia! And, uh, where are you going today?

Boys: Big Apple Tours!

Boy 1: We're going on, like, a double-decker bus, like that.

Reporter: Where is it going to take you?

Boys: All over New York . . . west Manhattan and the Empire State Building . . . Harlem.

Reporter: Empire State Building. What else do you want to go see?

Boy 2: Statue of Liberty.

Boy 1: And *that* is our bus.

Reporter: Here comes your bus. All right. Well, get on your bus, and thank you very much. Have a great time.

Boy 1: No problem.

• • •

Reporter: Me? I'm just going to have a hot dog and watch all the people go by. This is Chuck Santoro, reporting from New York City.

12 The doctor and the patient

Mr. Lewis, who is sick, goes to see the doctor and ends up solving the doctor's health problem.

Receptionist: Mr. Lewis?

Mr. Lewis: Yes.

Receptionist: The doctor will see you now.

• • •

Dr. North: Come in. Mr. Lewis. How are you?

Mr. Lewis: Fine, thanks.

Dr. North: What's the problem today?

Mr. Lewis: It's my ear. I have an earache.

Dr. North: Well, let's have a look. Please sit down over here. Is it the right ear or the left?

Mr. Lewis: It's the right one.

Dr. North: OK now. Let's see. Mmm. Yes. . . . Yep. Do you swim, Mr. Lewis?

Mr. Lewis: Yes, I do. I swim every morning.

Dr. North: Well, I'm going to give you these ear drops . . . and some pills.

Mr. Lewis: Thanks, Doctor.

Dr. North: Take the pills every day for a week. Use the drops every morning. And don't swim for a week.

Mr. Lewis: And then?

Dr. North: And then you can swim again. Come back and see me if you have . . . mmm!

Mr. Lewis: Dr. North? Are you OK?

Dr. North: No. Oh, it's my back.

Mr. Lewis: Don't worry, Doctor. I can help.

Dr. North: You can?

Mr. Lewis: Yes, I can. You see, my father has a bad back and I help him all the time. I'm very good at this. Here. . . . How's that?

Dr. North: Much better. Oh, thank you.

Mr. Lewis: Now, Doctor, lie down on the table.

Dr. North: Lie down?

Mr. Lewis: Yes. Right here.

Dr. North: OK.

Mr. Lewis: Now, bend your knees and put your feet up on the table.

Dr. North: Like this?

Mr. Lewis: Yes, that's right. . . . Now bring your right knee up to your chest. . . . Good. . . . And now your left knee. . . . Very good.

• • •

Nurse: Where is Dr. North? He's late.

Receptionist: Oh, he's with Mr. Lewis in Room B. Just a moment. (*using intercom*) Dr. North?

Mr. Lewis: Yes?

Receptionist: Are you . . . ready for your next patient?

Mr. Lewis: Um, no. . . . The doctor's –

Dr. North: Fine.

Receptionist: Doctor?

Dr. North: (*to Mr. Lewis*) I'm fine, thanks! (*to nurse*) Who's the next patient?

13 A visit to Mount Rushmore

A young couple tries to get to one of the United States's most famous monuments – before the sun goes down.

Susan: All right. I think that's everything. Are you ready to go?

Jim: I think so. Um . . . wait.

Susan: What?

Jim: Where's the map?

Susan: What map?

Jim: The map to Mount Rushmore.

Susan: I don't have a map.

Jim: Well, me neither.

Susan: Well, we can buy one at a gas station. Let's go!

Jim: First, we need film.

Susan: Not now. We can get some later. Let's go. OK? It's already three o'clock. I want to see Mount Rushmore.

Jim: OK, let's go.

• • •

Jim: Excuse me. Do you have any maps?

Attendant: Maps to . . .

Jim: To Mount Rushmore.

Attendant: No, but I can give you directions.

Jim: Great!

Attendant: Do you want the scenic route?

Jim: Uh, sure. Sure, that sounds great.

Attendant: OK. Take Highway 44 west, out of town.

Susan: OK.

Attendant: Then turn left on 385.

Jim: Highway 385.

Attendant: Uh-huh. Then take 244 east, and follow the signs to Mount Rushmore.

Jim: OK. Thanks a lot.

Susan: Yeah, thanks.

Jim: How far is it?

Attendant: It's about fifty miles.

Jim: Fifty miles. Thanks. . . . Do you have any film?

Attendant: No, but you can get some at the convenience store right across the street.

Jim: Thanks.

Susan: Oh, right. Film.

Jim: I'll get it. . . . OK, here's the film.

Susan: Great! We can get some good photos in this light. Let's hurry.

Jim: Uh, Susan? I'm kind of hungry.

Susan: Hungry?

Jim: Yeah. Can we stop and get something to eat?

Susan: Jim!

Jim: Something quick. Some fast food.

Susan: OK.

Jim: All right. Just a minute. . . . Excuse me. Is there a fast-food restaurant near here?

Attendant: Yeah, there's a place on Main. If you go up to the red light, turn left, and go three blocks, you can't miss it.

Jim: Thanks. . . . OK. Now let's go to Mount Rushmore.

Susan: I hope we get there before dark. It's already four o'clock!

Jim: Oh, don't worry.

Susan: What's the road?

Jim: Highway 44. We take it east out of town.

Susan: East?

Jim: Yeah, east.

• • •

Susan: Jim, I think we're going the wrong way.

Jim: Um, I think you're right. . . . What time is it?

Susan: About five-thirty.

Jim: There's 385.

Susan: And we're going to turn . . .

Jim: Left.

Susan: Are you sure?

Jim: Yeah, . . . I'm sure.

Susan: No, I think it's right.

(continued)

Jim: Right?

Susan: Yeah, I'm sure. Right. . . .

Jim: Oh, . . .

Susan: What, Jim?

Jim: We're lost.

Susan: I know. . . . This isn't right. Where's 244?

Jim: I don't know.

Susan: Let's go back.

• • •

Susan: There's a sign!

Jim: And there it is!

Susan: Where? I can't see anything.

Jim: So, . . . let's come back tomorrow?

Susan: Yeah, why not? Now we know how to get here.

During lunch, Rick tells George about his disastrous weekend.

George: Hi, Rick. How was your weekend?

Rick: My weekend? It was terrible!

George: Really? What happened?

Rick: Do you really want to know?

George: Of course.

Rick: Well, on Saturday, my mom and dad went away for the day.

George: Yeah?

. . .

Rick's mother: There's a pizza in the refrigerator.

Rick: Uh-huh.

Rick's father: And here's the number at Aunt Helen's.

Rick: Thanks, Dad.

Rick's mother: Cook the pizza for fifteen minutes.

Rick's father: See you at eleven tonight.

Rick's mother: And don't burn it.

Rick: OK. All right. See you tonight. Bye.

. . .

George: So, what happened?

Rick: Well, they left at one o'clock, and I was hungry.

George: Uh-huh.

Rick: So I put a pizza in the oven.

George: Yeah?

Rick: And then I called Julia on the phone. We talked for about an hour.

George: Uh-oh.

Rick: Uh-oh is right. . . .

George: So what did you do?

Rick: I ran back upstairs, and I called the fire department.

. . .

Rick: Yes, 2525 Perry Avenue. Fire! Hurry!

. . .

George: Did a fire truck come?

Rick: Yes, it did. And the firemen put the fire out.

George: Oh. Well, that's good.

Rick: No, that's *bad*. There was water all over the kitchen. . . .

Kate: Did you clean it up?

Rick: Yeah, I cleaned it up. It took two hours – from two to four o'clock.

George: So, then what did you do?

Rick: Do you really want to know?

George: Of course!

Rick: Well, I was really hungry.

George: Uh-huh.

Rick: So I went to the store to get a pizza.

George: Yeah?

Rick: And I drove there in my dad's new car.

George: Oh no!

Rick: Oh, yes. I got back, and guess what! I drove the car into the garage door. . . .

George: Oh! Was your father angry?

Rick: Well, my parents came home late that night, but the next day . . .

George: And what about your mother?

Rick: She thanked me.

George: She *thanked* you?

Rick: Yeah! She said, "The kitchen . . . it's so clean!"

George: Well, anyway, that's good. So what did you do on Sunday?

Rick: I found a part-time job . . . at the pizza shop.

George: The pizza shop? You?

Rick: Yeah! Garage doors are expensive, George. And I need the money.

George: Well, cheer up, Rick. I'll buy you an ice cream.

Rick: Gee, thanks, George. . . . So, George, how was *your* weekend?

George: Oh, my weekend was fantastic! First, . . .

15 Hollywood then and now

After we hear a short history of the movie industry, young people talk about their dreams of success in Hollywood.

Jim: Arnold Schwarzenegger . . . Marilyn Monroe . . . Eddie Murphy . . . Elizabeth Taylor. . . . This is Hollywood. . . . Hi, my name is Jim Hodson, and today we're in Hollywood, California, the home of American movies then and now. American movies are popular throughout the world. But how did it all start? . . . Well, moviemaking actually began back in 1903. The movie was *The Great Train Robbery.* . . . Early movies were in black and white. They had no sound. People watched the movie and read the story. A piano player played along with the movie. . . . In 1927, *The Jazz Singer* changed everything. It was the first movie with sound. . . . Then, in 1939, *Gone With the Wind* changed everything again. It was the first movie in color. . . . Hollywood made hundreds of movies every year. . . . A few of these movies became classics. And a few actors and actresses became stars. . . . Today Hollywood is still the home of American movies, and each year people come to Hollywood from all over the country and the world. Many of them come as tourists, but some have dreams. They want to be stars, and they come to Hollywood to find a job in the movies. Let's talk with some of them.

•   •   •

Jim: Well, what's your name?

Woman 1: Hi. I'm Rocky.

Jim: Rocky. Where are you from?

Woman 1: Northern California . . . Monterey.

Jim: When did you come to southern California?

Woman 1: I came down here in '87 to go to school.

Jim: And what was your major?

Woman 1: Communications.

•   •   •

Jim: Hi. What is your name?

Man 1: Hi. Brian Rupert.

Jim: Brian, where are you from?

Man 1: Iowa.

Jim: Iowa?

Man 1: Yep. Sioux City, Iowa.

Jim: Very nice. When did you move here?

Man 1: Two and a half years ago.

Jim: *Why* did you move here?

Man 1: To get into movies.

Jim: Really? As an actor?

Man 1: Yes.

Jim: Do you have another job?

Man 1: Security guard.

•   •   •

Jim: Hi. What's your name?

Man 2: My name is Brian Holdman.

Jim: And where are you from?

Man 2: I'm originally from Denver, Colorado.

Jim: Denver, ah, and why did you come to Los Angeles?

Man 2: Uh, well, I wanted to get a job in the entertainment business.

Jim: Ah. Did you?

Man 2: Yeah, I did.

•   •   •

Jim: And what is your name?

Woman 2: Rebecca McFarland.

Jim: And where are you from?

Woman 2: I'm from New Orleans . . . Louisiana.

Jim: And why did you come here?

Woman 2: To be an actress . . . I did.

Jim: Is it going well?

Woman 2: It's going extremely well.

•   •   •

Jim: Uh, what's your name?

Woman 3: Gina.

Jim: Um, and where are you from?

Woman 3: Cincinnati, Ohio.

Jim: Cincinnati. And when did you move here?

Woman 3: In June, just about, what, four months ago, I guess.

Jim: Wow. And why did you move here?

Woman 3: I moved here to try to get into film production, video production.

· · ·

Jim: Hi. What's your name?

Man 3: Hi, my name is Roberto Bakalski.

Jim: And where are you from?

Man 3: I'm from San Diego, California.

Jim: When did you move to Los Angeles?

Man 3: Uh, about six, seven months ago.

Jim: Oh, really? And why did you come here?

Man 3: To be an actor.

Jim: Do you study acting?

Man 3: Yeah, I'm studying with a teacher right here in Studio City.

Jim: What is your job here in L.A. as you study?

Man 3: I've got two jobs to pay the bills.

Jim: Thanks for talking with us. Good luck to you.

Man 3: Thanks a lot.

· · ·

Jim: Remember the names and faces you saw today. Maybe someday you'll see them again . . . in the movies. I'm Jim Hodson, live from Hollywood.

16 The perfect date

When Kate has more dating opportunities than she can handle, she learns that honesty is the best policy.

Ben: So, Kate, it's the weekend. What are you going to do?

Kate: I don't know. I really want to go to the Spiders concert, but I need a ticket. And Maggie's having a party, but –

Ben: But?

Kate: But I don't want to go. I can't. Dan's going to call.

Ben: Dan?

Kate: Yeah. He's this great guy in my art class.

Ben: But what happened to Greg? And Tony?

Kate: Oh, Greg? He's boring. And Tony? I don't know. He's kind of . . .

Ben: [*phone rings*] Maybe that's Dan.

Kate: Don't answer it. Wait!

Answering machine: We can't come to the phone right now. So please leave your name and phone number after the beep. We'll call you back soon.

Maggie: (*leaving message*) Hi, Kate. This is Maggie. I'm going to have a small party at my house tonight.

Ben: Kate!

Maggie: (*leaving message*) Do you want to come?

Kate: [*picking up phone*] Hi, Maggie. How are you?

Maggie: Oh, Kate! Hi. Fine, thanks. Listen, I'm going to have a small party at my house tonight. Do you want to come?

Kate: Oh, Maggie, I'd love to come, but . . . I have a really bad cold.

Maggie: Oh, that's too bad. I hope you feel better.

Kate: Thanks, Maggie. Bye. . . . [*phone rings*] Ben, no!

Ben: Don't worry. [*picks up phone*] Hello?

Greg: Hi. This is Greg. Is Kate there?

Ben: Just a moment. (*to Kate*) It's Greg. Are you home?

Kate: I guess. (*takes phone*) Hi, Greg.

Greg: Hi, Kate. What are you doing?

Kate: Studying. Why?

Greg: Well, Maggie's going to have a party tonight. Do you want to go?

Kate: Uh, gee, Greg, I can't. I have to study. You know me. I need to study.

Greg: Oh, well . . .

Kate: Sorry, Greg. Thanks. Bye.

Greg: Bye, Kate.

Kate: [*phone rings*] Hello?

Tony: Hi, Kate?

Kate: Yes?

Tony: It's Tony.

Kate: Oh. . . . Hi, Tony. How are you?

Tony: I'm great! Uh, listen. There's a party at Maggie's tonight. Do you want to go?

Kate: A party? Gee, Tony, I don't think so. I just, um, started a new book!

Tony: A new book?

Kate: Yeah, I'm reading it right now! Maybe next time?

Tony: OK, Kate. See you.

Kate: Sorry.

Ben: A new book? [*phone rings*] I'm not going to answer it.

Answering machine: We can't come to the phone right now, so please leave your name and phone number after the beep. We'll call you back soon.

Dan: Hi, Kate? This is Dan Saunders. I'm in your art class and . . .

Kate: [*picking up phone*] Dan? Hi. This is Kate. How are you?

Dan: I'm great. Kate, Maggie's brother just gave me two tickets to the Spiders concert. Do you want to go?

Kate: The Spiders concert? I'd love to go.

Dan: That's fantastic! Listen, I'm at Maggie's. Can you meet me here?

Kate: At Maggie's?

Dan: Right. I'm at Maggie's. The concert starts at nine o'clock, so let's meet at eight. We can go to the concert from here.

Kate: At Maggie's? At eight o'clock?

Dan: Yes, at Maggie's. She's having a party . . .

Authors' Acknowledgments

A great number of people assisted in the development of the *Interchange* and *New Interchange* videos. Particular thanks go to the following:

The **reviewers** for their helpful suggestions:

Lisa Baker, Andrew Harper, Susan Neumeier, Chuck Sandy, and Marcel Van Amelsvoort (Intro level)

Valerie A. Benson, Julie Dyson, Dorien Grunbaum, Cynthia Hall Kouré, Mark Kunce, Peter Mallett, Pamela Rogerson-Revell, Chuck Sandy, and Jody Simmons (Level One)

Steve Copley, Fergus MacKinnon, Jay Melton, and Chuck Sandy (Level Two)

The **students** and **teachers** in the following schools and institutes who pilot-tested the Video or Video Activity Book; their valuable comments and suggestions helped shape the content of the entire program:

Athenée Français, Tokyo, Japan; **Centro Cultural Brasil-Estados Unidos**, Belém, Brazil; **Eurocentres**, Virginia, U.S.A.; **Fairmont State College**, West Virginia, U.S.A.; **Hakodate Daigaku**, Hokkaido, Japan; **Hirosaki Gakuin Daigaku**, Aomori, Japan; **Hiroshima Shudo Daigaku**, Hiroshima, Japan; **Hokkaido Daigaku, Institute of Language and Cultural Studies**, Hokkaido, Japan; **The Institute Meguro**, Tokyo, Japan; **Instituto Brasil-Estados Unidos**, Rio de Janeiro, Brazil; **Instituto Cultural de Idiomas**, Caxias do Sul, Brazil; **Musashino Joshi Daigaku**, Tokyo, Japan; **Nagasaki Gaigo Tanki Daigaku**, Nagasaki, Japan; **New Cida**, Tokyo, Japan; **Parco-ILC English School**, Chiba, Japan; **Pegasus Language Services**, Tokyo, Japan; **Poole Gakuin Tanki Daigaku**, Hyogo, Japan; **Seinan Gakuin Daigaku**, Fukuoka, Japan; **Shukugawa Joshi Tanki Daigaku**, Hyogo, Japan; **Tokai Daigaku**, Kanagawa, Japan; **YMCA Business School**, Kanagawa, Japan; and **Yokohama YMCA**, Kanagawa, Japan.

On Intro Video and the accompanying print materials, the following **editorial** and **production** team:

Sylvia P. Bloch, John Borrelli, Karen Davy, Andrew Gitzy, Deborah Goldblatt, Emma Gordon, Pauline Ireland, James R. Morgan, Kathy Niemczyk, Howard Siegelman, and Mary Vaughn.

And Cambridge University Press **staff** and **advisors**:

Carlos Barbisan, Will Capel, Riitta da Costa, Peter Davison, Kyoko Fukunaga, David Harrison, Carine Mitchell, Chuanpit Phalavadhana, Helen Sandiford, Dan Schulte, Kumiko Sekioka, Ian Sutherland, Craig Walker, Janaka Williams, and Ellen Zlotnick.

And a special thanks to the video producer, Master Communications Group.